MARJORIE HOPE NICOLSON

The Breaking of the Circle

STUDIES

IN THE EFFECT OF THE "NEW SCIENCE"

UPON SEVENTEENTH-CENTURY POETRY

Revised Edition

Columbia University Press, New York & London

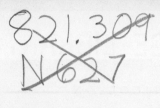
For *Ross Lee Finney*
in whose Spherical Madrigals
echoes again the charm of
the Circle of Perfection

First Edition Published by Northwestern University Press
Copyright © 1960 Columbia University Press, New York
Revised Edition
Columbia Paperback Edition 1962
Third printing and second paperback printing 1965
Manufactured in the United States of America

PREFACE

The first edition of this volume was an amplification of the Norman Wait Harris Lectures delivered at Northwestern University in July, 1949. The substance of the four lectures is largely contained in Chapters 1, 2, 4, and 5. As I pointed out in my original Preface, Chapter 1, "A Little World Made Cunningly," pretends to be little more than a recapitulation of materials familiar to students and scholars of the seventeenth century. It parallels E. M. W. Tillyard's *The Elizabethan World Picture*, though I concern myself primarily with the idea of macrocosm and microcosm, which Mr. Tillyard treats only as one among several prevalent conceptions. My purpose was much the same as that suggested in Mr. Tillyard's Preface in which he indicated that, when he was writing his larger work on Shakespeare's history plays, he came to realize that "the picture of civil war and disorder they present had no meaning apart from a background of order to judge them by," and that that order was "much more than political order, or, if political, was always a part of a larger cosmic order." With Mr. Tillyard, I believe that we must understand basic Renaissance preconceptions about man, the world, and the universe if we are fully to appreciate the art of the Renaissance poets.

In the original lectures I did not include my interpretation of Donne's *Anniversary Poems*, which appears here and in the first edition as Chapter 3, because such analysis depends upon a close study of the text and would not have been intelligible to a general audience. As I anticipated, this section of my book has proved the most provocative to critics. I was aware that I would not persuade Sir Herbert Grierson by my arguments about the spelling of "she" and "shee," since we had discussed the matter before I published the first edition of *The Breaking of the Circle*, and I knew that he had found it impossible to reach any definitive conclusion about the double "e" in his long study of various seventeenth-century texts, particularly those of Milton. I appreciate the careful attention he gave to my book in *Modern Language Review*, XLVII (1952), 320–22, and shall remember with affection that he corresponded with me more than once about the matter—among the last letters he must have written. I am grateful, too, to Joan Bennett for her analysis of this and other problems in *The Review of English Studies*, N. S. III (1952), 178–80, particularly in her suggestion that the spelling of "shee" was intended to indicate metrical stress on the syllable rather than to suggest the "Idea of a Woman."

At about the time I was preparing my book for the press, Marius Bewley was writing an article on the *Anniversary Poems*, which was published under the title "Religious Cynicism in Donne's Poetry" in the *Kenyon Review*, XIV (1952), 609–46. Approaching the problem from quite different grounds, Mr. Bewley also suggested the identification of some passages in the *Anniversaries* with the Virgin Queen. Louis Martz has replied to both of us in *The Poetry of Meditation* (New Haven, 1954), Appendix 2, pp. 353–56, interpreting some of the passages cited by Mr. Bewley and me as referring to a recent death, rather than to one that had occurred in 1603. I am more than willing to grant that various passages in the *Anniversary Poems* refer to the death of Elizabeth Drury, but am still persuaded that those I have particularly stressed refer to Queen Elizabeth. If I have persisted in my interpretations of "shee," it does not mean, I assure these various critics, that I have not considered their replies with great care. If I have not persuaded them, they have not persuaded me. As Donne himself said in a very different context:

> And one Soule thinkes one, and another way
> Another thinkes. . . .

Whether I may conclude with him that " 'tis an even lay," I must leave to still other critics.

Since this book originally appeared, I have published *Mountain Gloom and Mountain Glory* (Cornell University Press, 1959), upon which I was working before and after I gave the Norman Wait Harris Lectures. In my notes to the first edition I suggested that *The Breaking of the Circle* took its departure from some ideas with which I had dealt in the Messenger Lectures at Cornell University in 1949 under the title "The Sublime in External Nature." In *Mountain Gloom and Mountain Glory* I have more fully treated some of the conceptions that were still embryonic in my mind when I gave the lectures at Northwestern, particularly "The Aesthetics of the Infinite." As I have suggested in my Preface to *Mountain Gloom and Mountain Glory*, there is some overlapping with this volume, particularly in Chapter 4. There is also a slight amount of duplication in my passing treatment here of Shakespeare and Marlowe in Chapter 5 and one section in another of my books which has appeared since the first edition of this work, *Science and Imagination* (Cornell University Press, 1956), pp. 41–44. Since the ideas treated in this brief section are significant in connection with both subjects, I have allowed the duplication to stand.

As I have suggested in various notes, in this revised version I have had the added assistance of certain works of scholarship and criticism which have appeared since the first edition of this work, patricularly the valuable articles of Joseph Mazzeo to which I refer in the Introduction, which further develop the conception of universal analogy as a clue to the metaphysical poetic. I have also had the benefit of R. C. Bald's careful study of the Drury family, based upon unpublished manuscripts in the library of the University of Chicago, published as *Donne and the Drurys* (Cambridge, 1959). Professor Bald has been able to speak with more authority than any previous scholar upon such matters as the date of composition of the *Anniversary Poems* and Donne's relationship with Sir Robert Drury, which until his study of the manuscripts remained largely conjecture.

In my quotations from the seventeenth-century writers, I have used the following editions: *The Works of Sir Thomas Browne,* ed. by Geoffrey Keynes (London, 1928–31); *The Poems of Richard Crashaw,* ed. by L. C. Martin (Oxford, 1957; 1st ed., 1927); *Poetical Works of Giles and Phineas Fletcher,* ed. by Frederick S. Boas (Cambridge, 1908); *The Works of George Herbert,* ed. by F. E. Hutchinson (Oxford, 1945); *The Poems and Letters of Andrew Marvell,* ed. by H. M. Margoliouth (Oxford, 1927); *The Poetical Works of John Milton,* ed. by David Masson (London and New York, 1903); *The Poetical Works of Thomas Traherne,* ed. by Glayds I. Wade (London, 1932); *Centuries of Meditaﾷions,* ed. by Bertram Dobell (London, 1927); *The Works of*

Henry Vaughan, ed. by Leonard Cyril Martin (Oxford, 1914). In cases of other authors, specific references have been included in the accompanying footnotes.

I may conclude by saying, as in the first edition, that I offer no apology for what may seem an excessive amount of quotation from the seventeenth-century poets and from Sir Thomas Browne, who belongs with his fellow-poets. My desire was not to read my own theories into most of them (with the exception of Donne in the *Anniversary Poems*), but to let them speak for themselves and tell us in their own words how they looked at the universe, the world, and man. If I had a secondary reason for quoting, it was a selfish one. This book was originally intended as a series of lectures. There is no purer pleasure than that of reading aloud some of the most charming verses and phrases our literature has ever known.

MARJORIE HOPE NICOLSON

*Columbia University
in the City of New York
May, 1960*

CONTENTS

INTRODUCTION

Looking back with historical perspective, modern critics draw sharp lines of demarcation between three main epochs in European thought; the classical, the post-Renaissance, and the modern. Each of these had its own way of thinking about man, the world, and the universe. "Greek natural science," writes R. G. Collingwood in *The Idea of Nature*,[1] "was based on the principle that the world of nature is saturated or permeated by mind. . . . Since the world of nature is a world not only of ceaseless motion and therefore alive, but also a world of orderly or regular motion, they accordingly said that the world of nature is not only alive but intelligent; not only a vast animal with a 'soul' or 'life,' but a rational animal with a 'mind' of its own." From the time of Thales down through the period we broadly call "the Renaissance," a majority of philosophers taught and most men believed that the world was animate. It lived and flourished as did man, and like man was susceptible of decay, even of death.

During the seventeenth century the old hylozoistic fallacy gave way to the idea of the world as mechanism. "The Renaissance view of nature began to take shape as antithetical to

[1] R. G. Collingwood, *The Idea of Nature* (New York and Oxford, 1960), pp. 3–9.

the Greek view in the work of Copernicus, Telesio, and Bruno. The central point of this antithesis was the denial that the world of nature, the world studied by physical science, is an organism, and the assertion that it is devoid both of intelligence and of life. . . . Instead of being an organism, the natural world is a machine: a machine in the literal and proper sense of the word, an arrangement of bodily parts designed and put together and set going for a definite purpose by an intelligent mind outside itself." The world-machine was no longer animate, but mechanically responsive to the laws of Nature.

In more modern times, man passed from a conception of mechanism to one of development. "Modern cosmology, like its predecessors," Mr. Collingwood continues, "is based on an analogy. What is new about it is that the analogy is a new one. As the Greeks' natural science was based on the analogy between the macrocosm nature and the microcosm man, . . . as Renaissance natural science was based on the analogy between nature as God's handiwork and the machines that are the handiwork of man, . . . so the modern view of nature . . . is based on the analogy between the processes of the natural world as studied by natural scientists and the vicissitudes of human affairs as studied by historians."

Modern cosmology, like all the earlier ones, is based on analogy. But we are aware that it is an analogy. We know that we are attempting to explain the nature of the universe, the world, and man by figures of speech deliberately drawn from historians and natural scientists. We describe our world in similes. Our Elizabethan ancestors thought of their world in metaphors. The world was not simply *like* an animal; it *was* animate. The repetition of pattern, design, function they found in the body of man was not invented by human ingenuity; it actually existed in the three worlds made by God in His image. There was basic correspondence between man's body and the body of the world, between man's soul and the soul of the universe.

Perhaps it was because he lived in an age of mechanism rather than animism that Samuel Johnson frequently misinterpreted the group of writers he called the "metaphysical poets." [2] His criticism is often just, so far as Cowley was concerned. A good deal is not true when applied to Donne and others now included in the "metaphysical" roster. In Johnson's mind, the first fault of these poets lay in what seemed their ostentatious learning. "As the authors of this race were perhaps more desirous of being admired than understood, they sometimes drew their conceits from recesses of learning not very much frequented by common readers of poetry. . . . The most heterogeneous ideas are yoked by violence together; nature and art are ransacked for illustrations, comparisons, and allusions; their learning instructs, and their subtilty surprises; but the reader commonly thinks his improvement dearly bought, and though he sometimes admires, he is seldom pleased." Johnson's second critique was basically one with the first. Avid for novelty, these poets "did not much inquire whether their allusions were to things high or low, elegant or gross. . . . Of thoughts so far fetched as to be not only unexpected but unnatural all their books are full." They seemed to Johnson to have racked their brains and exhausted their ingenuity in attempts to find new and startling comparisons. "They looked out not for images but for conceits," he said, and found them "by a voluntary deviation from nature in pursuit of something new and strange."

[2] Samuel Johnson, "Life of Cowley," in *Lives of the Poets*, ed. by G. B. Hill (Oxford, 1905), I, 19–22.

I should not labor a passage so familiar were it not that Johnson's shadow seems still to dim the eyes of various modern critics, both those who resurrected and almost deified Donne in the 1920s and 1930s and some who, going out with the ebbing tide of enthusiasm, now speak critically of the former idol. "All of us," Cleanth Brooks wrote in *The Well-Wrought Urn*,[3] "are familiar with the censure passed upon Donne and his followers by Dr. Johnson, and a great many of us still retain it as our own, softening only the rigor and thoroughness of its application, but not giving it up as a principle." It was no surprise to many of us who listened to the so-called "recantation" address on Milton that T. S. Eliot should have begun with the words, "Samuel Johnson . . . said. . . ."

The modern critics have often been more subtle than Johnson, and they have used a vocabulary that would have puzzled the Dictionary-Maker, interpreting in terms of "paradox," "irony," "ambiguity," "ambivalence," "tension." They have frequently shown more interest in Donne's "logic" than in his poetry. Although they have analyzed in closer detail such "illustrations, comparisons, and allusions" as those that provoked Johnson to his strictures, many still believe that the essential element of metaphysical poetry lay in a kind of intellectual perverseness, that Donne and his followers deliberately yoked together by violence the most heterogeneous ideas in order to form a *discordia concors*. In effect they seem to say of Donne as Samuel Butler of Hudibras:

> For rhetorick he could not ope
> His mouth, but out there flew a trope.

Although the modern critics more often praised than condemned him for the fact, they insisted that some of Donne's

[3] Cleanth Brooks, *The Well-Wrought Urn* (New York, 1947), p. 212.

finest figures were "conceits" rather than "images," produced, as Johnson believed, "by a voluntary deviation from nature in pursuit of something new and strange."

To be sure, many of the seventeenth-century poets were learned, though their learning did not seem as ostentatious to their own age as to Johnson's and our own. They were witty poets, too, in all the senses in which their own generation understood wit, and in which Addison both praised and condemned their use of it. But many of the supposed conceits Johnson and they cited were not so novel and strange as they thought. Indeed, the figures were often not conceits but metaphors, drawn from a pattern of the universe which seemed to the poets inevitable, in which the little body of man corresponded exactly to the larger body of the world, and that in turn to the still larger body of the universe, in which "the elements that do man's house compose" were the same elements—earth, water, air, fire—that composed the body of the world and the body of the universe. The pattern of the three interlocking worlds was not invented or discovered by poets, avid for novelty. It was inscribed upon man, world, and universe in which design, plan, and repetition of motif were everywhere apparent.[4] Many of their basic figures of speech which Johnson and some modern critics misunderstood were drawn directly and inevitably from a Nature we have long forgotten.

As critics have either blamed or praised the seventeenth-

[4] Since the first edition of this book appeared, the relationship between the idea of universal analogy and metaphysical poetry has been developed by Joseph Mazzeo in a series of important articles: "A Seventeenth-Century Theory of Metaphysical Poetry," *Romanic Review*, XLII (1951), 245–55; "A Critique of Some Modern Theories of Metaphysical Poetry," *Modern Philology*, L (1952), 88–96; "Metaphysical Poetry and the Poetry of Correspondence," *Journal of the History of Ideas*, XIV (1953), 221–34; "Universal Analogy and the Culture of the Renaissance," *ibid.*, XV (1954), 299–304.

century poets for the perverseness or brilliance of some supposed "novel" figures that were actually Renaissance common-
places, so they missed others that were really new when Donne
and his contemporaries wrote.[5] Certainly there are comparisons in the poetry of the earlier seventeenth century for
which we find no parallels in Chaucer or Spenser or even
Shakespeare. The images were new. The poets did not rack
their brains or ransack Nature to invent them. They burst
around them as bombs around our own atomic age. We can
no longer think as our ancestors thought. We can merely try
to understand their belief in the three worlds of an animate
Nature and sympathetically to appreciate the delight they felt
as they found everywhere fresh proof of the design of a
"metaphysical" God in the intricate repetitive patterns of
man, the world, and the universe, in "correspondence" and
"signature," in the "mystical Mathematicks" loved by Sir
Thomas Browne that stirred Kepler to rapture when he discovered that Plato's five regular solids afford the clue to the
relationship among the planets. Delight in mathematics led
Marvell to think of lovers in terms of parallel lines that never
meet, Donne to describe them as a pair of compasses, and
Milton to use the same symbol when in one of his most reverent scenes in *Paradise Lost* he imagined the creation of the
world by the Son of God:

> He took the golden compasses, prepared
> In God's eternal store, to circumscribe
> The Universe and all created things.

[5] Had Johnson better understood the basic presuppositions of Donne's
age, he would not have thought the "balsamum" reference learned nor
Donne's "reflection upon Man as a Microcosm . . . abstruse and profound."
On the other hand, had his age realized what was really new in Donne's
he would hardly have said, "Who but Donne would have thought that a
good man is a telescope," or found "confusion worse confounded" in
Donne's figures of the "she sun" and the "he moon."

One foot he centered, and the other turned
Round through the vast profundity obscure,
And said, "Thus far extend, thus far thy bounds;
This be thy just circumference, O World"

(*PL*, vii.225–31)

"Modern cosmology, like its predecessors, is based on an analogy." The cosmology of the Renaissance poets, as we shall see, was most often interpreted in terms of the circle—a circle that existed in the perfect spheres of the planets, in the circular globe, in the round head of man. This was not mere analogy to them; it was truth. God had made all things in the universe, the world, and the body of man as near his own symbol, the perfect circle, as their grosser natures would allow. Older theories of history, when they were not degenerative, had been cyclical. Sir Thomas Browne said: "The Lives, not only of Men, but of Commonwealths, and the whole World, run not upon an Helix that still enlargeth, but on a Circle, where, arriving to their Meridian, they decline in obscurity, and fall under the Horizon again."

What once seemed "identicals" have become in our modern world only "similars." Metaphor, based upon accepted truth, inscribed by God in the nature of the universe, has given way to simile. But much more than that, we shall see, is involved in the circle. Why did this metaphor, the most persistent and the most loved metaphor of earlier writers, almost disappear from literature for more than a century? Why, when it returned, did it tend to be "conceit" rather than "image"? The Circle of Perfection, from which man for so long deduced his ethics, his aesthetics, and his metaphysics, was broken during the seventeenth century. Correspondence between macrocosm, geocosm, and microcosm, long accepted as basic to faith, was no longer valid in a new mechanical world and mechanical universe, nor is it valid in the modern world.

During the nineteenth century, when the circle returned to literature, it tended, under the influence of the evolutionary theory and belief in progress, to be not the Circle of Perfection but a spiral, or what Sir Thomas Browne had called "an Helix that still enlargeth." As shades of the prison house have closed around the idea of progress, the circle has suffered still another change. "Things fall apart. The Centre cannot hold," said Yeats, in whose poetry the circle recurs perhaps more than in that of any other English poet. His is no closed circle but a spiral in which the movement is both upward and downward. In our times it would seem that we are approaching the end of a spiral. Yeats's circle was drawn from Vico, as is that of the other modern writer who has most used it in the structure of his work, James Joyce, who said in *Finnegans Wake:* "The Vico road goes round and round to meet where terms begin." [6] There may be variation but there is no progress—repetition, sometimes interruption, even degeneration. We cannot return to a world that died in the seventeenth century, nor feel as men felt when the circle was not a conceit but an image of reality, everywhere inscribed by God in the nature of things.

Even while Donne and his contemporaries were living in a universe of correspondences, other voices were beginning to be heard. "It is incredible," wrote Francis Bacon with his usual prosaic common sense, "what a number of idols have been introduced into philosophy by the reduction of natural operations to a correspondence with human actions, that is, by im-

---

[6] Quoted by William York Tindall, *James Joyce* (New York, 1959), p. 244. On Joyce's circle, see the same volume *passim*, also the chapter "Family Cycle in *Ulysses*," in Tindall, *James Joyce: His Way of Interpreting the Modern World* (New York, 1950). John Unterecker has discussed Yeats's spiral in *A Reader's Guide to William Butler Yeats* (New York, 1959), pp. 24–29.

agining that nature acts as man does, which is not much better than the heresy of anthropomorphists." To Bacon the Circle of Perfection was a mere fiction, and the inclination of men to find it everywhere on earth and in heaven another indication of the dangerous haziness be found in the "Idols of the Tribe." "The human understanding," he wrote, "is of its own nature prone to suppose the existence of more order and regularity in the world than it finds. And though there be many things in nature which are singular and unmatched, yet it devises for them conjugates and parallels and relatives which do not exist. Hence the fiction that all celestial bodies move in perfect circles." [7] As he inveighed against the almost universal tendency of his day to read nonexistent "conjugates and parallels and relatives" into Nature, so he opposed another idea of correspondence that we shall find pervasive in the literature of the earlier seventeenth century: the belief that the "humours" of man's body correspond to the four elements. Here again, as he said, men seemed to "make themselves, as it were, the mirror and rule of nature." And so, indeed, men did.

Baconian common sense was to triumph over mysticism. "Truth," he said, as if setting a motto for his eighteenth-century followers, "is a naked and open daylight." In the full blaze of the Enlightenment the Circle of Perfection disappeared, as Marvell's drop of dew when the sun rose. But Sir Thomas Browne, who felt as poets felt, seems to reply to Bacon: "Light that makes all things seen, makes some things

[7] *Novum Organum* XLV. In his earlier works Bacon occasionally used macrocosmic-microcosmic figures, though infrequently in comparison with most of his contemporaries. In his later work he consciously avoided the kind of analogical thinking he criticized in his generation, as may readily be seen by comparing the *De Augmentis Scientiarum* with the *Advancement of Learning*.

invisible. The greatest mystery of Religion is expressed by adumbration." Much more fully than Bacon, Browne understood an age when man sincerely believed that he was a little world made cunningly, a copy of his earth, as his earth was a copy of the universe, all three "epitomes" of God. Pondering upon one of his favorite figures, a favorite also of his generation, *Lux est Umbra Dei*, Browne said: "Where there is an obscurity too deep for our Reason, 'tis good to sit down with a description, periphrasis, or adumbration." [8] If we are to appreciate to its full the literature of the English Renaissance, we too must be willing to sit down with the "description, periphrasis, or adumbration" they used to explain obscurities too deep for Reason. We must come to think as they thought before "The Death of a World," before the animate macrocosm and living microcosm disappeared, and their places were taken by a mechanical clock and men with mechanical hearts.

[8] *Religio Medici*, I.10 (Keynes ed., I, 14).

"A LITTLE WORLD MADE CUNNINGLY"

"I am a little world made cunningly of elements," John Donne wrote in one of his most familiar devotional poems.[1] "Man is one world," said George Herbert, "and has another to attend him." [2] "Doe I not see in this blest earth heavens bright Epitome?" asked Crashaw.[3] Drummond of Hawthornden pondered: "Thou seemst a world in thyself, containing heaven, stars, earth, floods, mountains, forests and all that lives." [4] Was this mere rhetoric? If it tended to settle more and more into metaphor as the Renaissance wore on, truth still lay deep behind the phrases until the period of the Restoration.

To poets and prose-writers of the earlier seventeenth century, man *was* a little world made cunningly. At the Creation God had composed the universe of four elements—fire, air, water, earth; "then did of th' elements dust mans body frame, / A perfect microcosm." Milton was merely following tradition when he described the original chaos as it appeared to Satan at Hell-Gates:

[1] *Holy Sonnets*, v.   [2] *Man.*   [3] *Upon the King's Coronation.*
[4] *A Cypresse Grove*, in *Poems*, ed. by W. C. Ward (2 vols.; London, n.d. [1894]), II, 263.

> where eldest Night
> And Chaos, ancestors of Nature, hold
> Eternal anarchy, amidst the noise
> Of endless wars, and by confusion stand.
> For Hot, Cold, Moist, and Dry, four champions fierce,
> Strive here for mastery, and to battle bring
> Their embryon atoms.   (*PL*, ii.894–900)

Satan fought his way through "this wild Abyss, / The womb of Nature, and perhaps her grave,"

> Of neither Sea, nor Shore, nor Air, nor Fire,
> But all these in their pregnant causes mixt
> Confusedly, and which thus must ever fight,
> Unless the Almighty Maker them ordain
> His dark materials to create more worlds.   (*PL*, ii.912–16)

The original state of nature was a favorite theme with poets. Chapman wrote of the time before Creation,

> when unlightsome, vast, and indigest
> The formlesse matter of this world did lye. . . .
> When earth, the ayre, and sea in fire remain,
> When fire, the sea, and earth, the ayre containd;
> When sea, fire, ayre, in earth were indisposde.[5]

At the word of God, however, the elements settled into order:

> All things were one nothing, dull and weake,
> Until this raw disordered heape did breake,
> And severall desires led parts away:
> Water declin'd with earth, the ayre did stay,
> Fire rose, and each from other but unty'd,
> Themselves unprison'd were, and purify'd.[6]

[5] George Chapman, *Hymnus in Noctem*, in *Poems*, ed. by Phyllis Bartlett (New York, 1941), p. 20.
[6] John Donne, *To the Countesse of Huntingdon*.

For a time, amity and love prevailed among "the fighting parents of this universe":

> Fire, Water, Earth, and Aire (that fiercely strove)
> His soveraigne hand in strong alliance ti'd,
> Binding their deadly hate in constant love.[7]

If at first, as Marvell said in *Employment*, "the elements did for place contest with Him whose will / Ordained the highest to be best," at Creation they settled into that "order" taught by Milton's Angel to Adam:

> Of Elements
> The grosser feeds the purer: Earth the Sea,
> Earth and the Sea feed Air, the Air those Fires
> Ethereal, and, as lowest, first the Moon. . . .
> The Sun, that light imparts to all, receives
> From all his alimental recompense
> In humid exhalations, and at even
> Sups with the Ocean.   (*PL*, v.415–22)

The order of the elements, Adam learned, was repeated everywhere in nature: in the tree the root corresponded to earth, the green stalk to water, the leaves "more aerie" to air, the "bright consummate flower" to fire, toward which other elements aspired. Henry Vaughan in *The Tempest* phrased this "correspondence" in slightly different fashion:

> Plants in the root with Earth do most Comply,
>   Their Leafs with water and humiditie,
>   The Flowers to air draw neer, and subtiltie,
> And seeds a kindred fire have with the sky.

Like the universe, man too was framed of the four elements from which he came and to which he would return,

---

[7] Phineas Fletcher, *The Purple Island*, I.41.

since "All which die / To their first Elements resolve." "Does not our life consist of the four elements?" asked Sir Toby Belch. In Adam, man believed, the elements had been perfectly combined. "Man in those early days / Was not all stone and earth." Since the Fall, however, man has suffered from elemental imbalance, at one time seeming all fire and spirit, at another a dull clod, earthbound and heavy, sometimes airy, sometimes volatile as water. Only on rare occasions could a Mark Antony say of a Brutus:

> His life was gentle, and the elements
> So mixed in him that Nature might stand up
> And say to all the world, "This was a *man!*"

Ordinarily, as Hamlet, Lear, Macbeth, Iago prove, such perfection of nature was as rare among Elizabethans as it is today, since

> The elements, that do man's house compose
>   Are all his chiefest foes;
> Fire, air, earth, water all are at debate,
>   Which shall predominate.[8]

Poets wrote lugubriously of

> My fire of Passion, sighes of ayre,
> Water of teares, and earthly sad despaire,
>   Which my materialls bee,

as did Donne in *The Dissolution,* or Marvell, who said of *The Unfortunate Lover:*

> The Sea him lent these bitter Tears,
> Which as his Eyes he alwaies bears.

---

[8] William Hammond, *On the Death of my Dear Brother,* in *Minor Poets of the Caroline Period,* ed. by George Saintsbury (3 vols.; Oxford, 1905, 1906, 1921), II, 513.

> And from the Winds the Sighs he bore,
> Which through his surging Breast do roar. . . .
> While Nature to his Birth presents
> That masque of quarelling Elements.

"Why do I languish thus, drooping and dull, / As if I were all earth?" lamented Herbert in *Dulnesse*. Looking about him in Nature, Vaughan in *The Tempest* felt that only man and man's element were out of harmony with the universe:

> All things here shew him heaven; Waters that fall,
>   Chide and fly up. . . .
>   trees, herbs, flowres, all
> Strive upwards stil, and point him the way home.

> How do they cast off grosness? only Earth
>   And man (like Issachar) in lodes delight,
>   Water's refin'd to Motion, Aire to Light,
> Fire to all three, but man hath no such mirth.

Like his earth, man was governed by the planets and stars. Saturnine or jovial, martial or mercurial, he was what cosmic forces had made him. "A star danced," laughed Beatrice, "and under that I was born." "Saturn was the lord of my geniture," said the Anatomist of Melancholy. As there were four elements, so there were four humors or fluids of man's physiological system, melancholy corresponding to earth, phlegm to water, blood to air, choler to fire. Had a man too much yellow bile, or choler, he would be choleric; had he too much black blood, or melancholy, he would temperamentally be a Hamlet. Our forefathers' placid acceptance of the theory of humors as predetermining man's nature seems at first quaint, even absurd, to modern students. They read their ancestors more sympathetically, I find, if by mere change of vocabulary they come to realize that "moderns" too believe that personalities are the result of imbalance. A few years ago it was easy to interpret the old theory of humors by analogy with "glands"—another catchword of another generation. There were few college classes in which one could not find a "hyperthyroid" or a "hypopituitary" who was convinced that his temperamental difficulties were the result of glandular over- or underactivity. Today—having advanced with the times— I take refuge in Webster (probably already out-of-date on the subject), and quote this definition: "*Gene:* An entity concerned with the transmission and development or determinant of hereditary characters; an element of the germ plasm; a factor, or determinant." Three centuries hence, I wonder, will we seem as naïve to our descendants, with our glands and our genes, as do our ancestors with their humors, their elements, and their "star-crossed lovers"?

There was nothing quaint about these ideas in the period of Shakespeare, who with more learned contemporaries accepted them as had Chaucer before him. The theory of the elements was still basic to Renaissance geology; the sciences of medicine and physiology were established on belief in the humors. Few physicians treated patients without first casting their horoscopes. Back of all these—elements, planets, humors —lay one central conception: belief in the interrelationship of the little world of man and the great world of the universe. So familiar is Shakespeare's treatment of that idea in the heath scene in *King Lear* that I almost hesitate to refer to it; yet because it *is* familiar, and because it is a poignant example of the interaction of two worlds, it serves as the best possible introduction to some aspects of the philosophical idea of macrocosm and microcosm, which was widely accepted when Shakespeare wrote. "Where's the King?" demanded Kent. A Gentleman replied:

Contending with the fretful elements;
Bids the wind blow the earth into the sea,
Or swell the curled waters 'bove the main,
That things might change or cease; tears his white hair,
Which the impetuous blasts, with eyeless rage,
Catch in their fury, and make nothing of;
Strives in his little world of man to out-scorn
The to-and-fro-conflicting wind and rain. (III.i)

When we ourselves see Lear on the heath, we realize that he is finding in the forces of nature the same imbalance we recognize in him:

Blow, winds, and crack your cheeks! rage! blow
You cataracts and hurricanoes . . .
        And thou, all-shaking thunder,
Strike flat the thick rotundity of the world!
Crack nature's moulds, all germens spill at once,
That make ungrateful man. (III.ii)

The elements have returned to their primitive state: earth, water, air, fire have reverted to their "deadly hate," each striving to usurp the place of the other in the universe. Into the winds, cataracts, and hurricanes Lear reads the battle of his own ungoverned passions. Is it he who "tears his white hair" or is it the storm-blasts, blind as Milton's Fury? The mad mind of Lear affects external nature, as the madness of nature affects Lear. Lear is losing his reason, Nature hers, and the one inevitably reacts upon the other. The microcosm reflects the macrocosm, the macrocosm the confusion in the little world, until neither we nor Lear can tell which is more responsible for the chaos.

Let us consider another Shakespearean scene, almost as familiar as the "mad scene" in *Lear*. The "Greek scene" in *Troilus and Cressida* still better illustrates the persistent

analogy of three worlds. Ulysses, seeking to explain why order is so necessary in the army, inevitably makes use of cosmic
analogy. Still accepting the old Ptolemaic astronomy, he takes
for granted that "the heavens themselves, the planets, and
this center" must "observe degree, priority, and place . . .
proportion, season, form." If at any time the planets "in evil
mixture" deserted their appointed places, the resulting chaos
and disorder would be reflected in earth-processes:

> What plagues and what portents, what mutiny,
> What raging of the sea, shaking of earth,
> Commotion in the winds, frights, changes, horrors,

would immediately occur in the terrestrial globe. In turn
chaos would be repeated in the economic and political world
of man, affecting the established order of

> primogenitive and due of birth,
> Prerogative of age, crowns, scepters, laurels.

Shakespeare's conclusions in *Lear* and *Troilus* were conventional statements of truths long taken for granted by men who
believed that "this center" was earth—the central sphere in
a concentric cosmos. Between Shakespeare's passages and John
Donne's *An Anatomie of the World*, in which Donne too
felt that because of universal chaos, "Prince, Subject, Father,
Sonne are things forgot," had occurred a revolution in human
thought, yet the central idea of the interaction of three worlds
is as clear in Donne as in Shakespeare. Indeed it is even more
apparent, since Donne and his later contemporaries, as we
shall see, were much more concerned about the nature of the
macrocosm than was Shakespeare, more concerned too with
man's relation to his earth as well as to his universe. Lear's
mad mind was aware of the madness of the elements, but
Lear did not lament, as will Henry Vaughan in *Repentance:*

> Oh, what am I, that I should breed
> Figs on a thorn, flowers on a weed!

Nor did Lear share Vaughan's feeling of guilt about man in general:

> He drew the Curse upon the world, and Crackt
> The whole frame with his fall.   (*Corruption*)

But these are still matters for the future. At the moment, it is enough to say that both the Elizabethans and the poets of the earlier seventeenth century took for granted three interlocking worlds, which somehow affected each other, and were particularly interested in the relation of the "little world of man" to the other two.

This habit of thinking in terms of universal analogy had a profound effect upon the advancement of science as we know it today. Psychology was involved in physiology. Medicine marked time while physicians sought to explain the structure of the human body by analogy with the structure of earth; geology was equally retarded while men read over into earth the processes and history of man. And both earth sciences and human sciences were greatly handicapped by the tendency to read into earth and man cosmic processes, and to find striking similarities between the body of man, the body of earth, "wandering" and "fixed" stars, and the shape and structure of the cosmic universe. Renaissance man who had discovered much about the geographical globe still knew little about the processes of his own body, as Donne suggested in *The Second Anniversary*:

> Knowst thou but how the stone doth enter in
> The bladders cave, and never breake the skinne?
> Know'st thou how blood, which to the heart doth flow,
> Doth from one ventricle to th' other goe?

And for the putrid stuffe, which thou dost spit,
Know'st thou how thy lungs have attracted it? . . .
What hope have wee to know our selves, when wee
Know not the least things, which for our use be?

During Donne's own lifetime, science was to answer some
of the questions that had puzzled man for centuries. But in
spite of Kepler and Gilbert and Harvey—indeed in part because of them, as we shall see—man continued to explain
human mysteries by analogies with the globe. As for the universe, that remained an even more insoluble riddle. All that
the human eye could discover about the nature of the cosmos
was known; the rest—even the theory of Copernicus—remained surmise. Into the globe, into the universe, man read
analogies drawn from his body, then read them back again
to explain his human mysteries. Earthbound in his finite
microcosm, his mind was free to roam into the macrocosm,
there to create new worlds, made in his own image:

The Mind, that Ocean where each kind
Does straight its own resemblance find;
Yet it creates, transcending these,
Far other Worlds, and other Seas.[9]

I

How old the idea of macrocosm and microcosm is, we can
not tell. Perhaps originally oriental, it appeared early among
Greek thinkers, who drew analogies between the "great
world" of the universe and the "little world" of man. It has
been called "Pythagorean" and "Platonic"—two terms which
have become convenient catch-alls. Certainly Plato had sug-

[9] Andrew Marvell, *The Garden.*

gested some aspects of the belief: parallels between man and
the state, such as he discussed in the *Republic;* emphasis upon
the "harmony of the universe," which man should copy if he
would find health and happiness; most of all—for my own
particular purposes in following the ways of that circle
which is my main theme—the mystical interlocking pattern
of creation in the *Timaeus:* the universe a great series of circles, the globe a lesser circle, the head of man, seat of human
reason, a little copy of the Great Circle in its roundness. The
Stoics had further developed implications of the macrocosm-
microcosm relationship. To them even more than to their
predecessors, the world was animate, even, some said, animal. The "world's body" lived, as did the "world soul." Like
man and like plants, it grew; like them it was subject to decay
and perhaps to death. Among the Alexandrians, particularly
through the influence of Philo Judaeus, oriental and occiden-
tal interpretations came together, with the result that,
throughout the Middle Ages, the macrocosm-microcosm conception was basic to many Jewish and Christian sages.

Never completely lost in Christian thinking, the idea developed powerfully during the Renaissance, and persisted
both in art and in literature. Otto Benesch, discussing Lucas
Cranach's *St. Jerome in Penitence,* says:

Painting realizes here for the first time in history what philosophy
established in the notion of the microcosm. The philosopher and
scientist meant by "microcosm" first of all man, who was supposed to mirror on a small scale everything that the macrocosm,
the universe, contains. This involves the fact that the macrocosm,
too, was considered as an organism. The smallest thing was in-
separably connected with the total, as in landscape art the fore-
ground is with the background by means of organic structure and
atmosphere. . . . The microcosm mirrors the macrocosm. This

relation became reality in the works of the early landscape painters.[10]

Agrippa, Pico della Mirandola, Nicholas of Cusa, Bruno, Campanella—these and many others adapted to the peculiarities of their own systems the macrocosm-microcosm conception. But none went so far as that extraordinary character, "Philippus Aureolus Theophrastus Paracelsus Bombast of Hohenheim," with whom John Donne had fun in *Ignatius his Conclave*, where he summoned him before the bar of Hell, with Copernicus and Machiavelli, as one of the "innovators" who had upset the world. For all his bombast Paracelsus had been an innovator and an important one, introducing new medicines such as opium, iron, arsenic, mercury, sulphur, and performing cures which seemed those of a magician rather than a physician. His teaching struck at the root of the theory of humors. In opposition to the Galenists, whose theories of medicine had been standard for centuries, he insisted that disease was not the result of disproportion of humors, to be corrected by herbal treatment opposing hot to cold, moist to dry. Disease was the result of imbalance of elements, which to Paracelsus were chiefly three: mercury, sulphur, salt. "Bad essences" in the body must be purged chemically. Donne, in one of his verse-letters to Sir Henry Wotton, was playing with the older and newer medical theories when he wrote:

> Onely in this one thing, be no Galenist; To make
> Courts hot ambition wholesome, do not take
> A dramme of Countries dulness; do not adde
> Correctives, but as chymiques, purge the bad.

Basic to all his treatments and medical theories was Paracelsus' belief in the complete correspondence of the body of

[10] Otto Benesch, *The Art of the Renaissance in Northern Europe* (Cambridge, Mass., 1945), p. 46.

man with the body of the world. "Man," he said, "is the lesser, and for his sake the Macrocosm, the greater world, was founded. . . . This therefore is the condition of the Microcosmus, or smaller world. It contains in its body all the minerals of the world. Consequently the body acquires its own medicine from the world. There is a vast variety of things contained in the body of the Microcosm which elude the observation of the senses, though God, the Creator, has willed them to exist in that structure. There are, for example, more than a thousand species of trees, stone, minerals, and metals. . . . Accordingly, know that the mysteries of the microcosm are to be mystically understood." [11] "Man is ev'ry thing, and more," said George Herbert. So Paracelsus believed: man *was* the elements; he was minerals and metals; he was fruit and trees, vegetables and flowers. He was also winds and storms and tempests.

"It is too little to call Man a little World," Donne wrote in Paracelsian strain in the *Devotions*. "Man consists of more pieces, more parts, than the World. . . . The whole world hath nothing, to which something in man doth not answere." He was almost paraphrasing Paracelsus when he wrote again: "Is this the honour which Man hath by being a little world, That he hath these earthquakes in him selfe, sodaine shakings; these lightnings, sodaine flashes; these thunders, sodaine noises; these Eclypses, sodaine offuscations, and darknings of his senses; these Blazing Stars, sodaine fiery exhalations; these Rivers of Blood, sodaine red waters?" [12]

"Nature," writes Otto Benesch, "was to Paracelsus a spiritual total which is reflected in every one of its parts. The aboriginal matter was to him the Mysterium Magnum, out of

[11] *The Hermetic and Alchemical Writings of Paracelsus*, trans. by Arthur E. Waite (London, 1894), I, 161.
[12] *Devotions upon Emergent Occasions*, Nos. IV, I.

which God shaped the world like an artist. The idea of the artist occurs again and again, and demonstrates Paracelsus' intuitive, artistic approach toward nature." In the paintings of Albrecht Altdorfer, Benesch finds many similarities to Paracelsian conceptions. As Paracelsus taught that the elements serve as matrix for various substances and that one substance merges into another, so in Altdorfer's panel of *St. John the Baptist and St. John the Evangelist*, "The cosmogonic landscape of the background shows steam rising from the sea, becoming smoke in the height, crystallizing to snowy mountains which dissolve again into wandering clouds. Rocks, cities, ships, grow like mineral formations out of the water. In a kind of picture alchemy, one form distils from the other." Of a little panel by Altdorfer, representing St. Jerome, Benesch says: "The figure seems to grow out of the earth like trees and plants. This is no metaphor. Paracelsus spoke of it clearly in his *Third Book of Philosophy*, when he compared plants with the human organism: 'This growth . . . is similar to man; it has the bark as its skin, the root as its head and hair; it has its body and senses; its sensibility in the stem, that it dies, if you hurt it.' " Considering another painting of Altdorfer, Benesch writes:

Paracelsus called the art of interpretation of nature "chiromancy." He applied it not only to the hands of men but also to plants, trees, woods, and finally even to scenery, through the means of mountains, roads, and rivers. The grandest chiromancy of scenery ever achieved by an artist is Albrecht Altdorfer's Battle of Alexander the Great against the Persian King Darius. . . . It unfolds a cosmic world panorama like the maps of the new cosmography. One color flows into the other; the elements, fire and water, fight in the air like men on earth. The fiery red and orange of the setting sun gilds the peaks of the gentian blue mountains; their chains circumscribe the vault of the earthly globe.

. . . Thus, Paracelsus wrote that the firmament is not of one complexion, but of many. . . . Altdorfer's colors are like those of the elementary substances described by Paracelsus: "They have no definite color, but many colors grow from them; they are composed from many colors." [13]

Francis Bacon declared impatiently: "The ancient opinion that man was *microcosmus*, an abstract or model of the world, hath been fantastically strained by Paracelsus and the alchemists, as if there were to be found in man's body certain correspondences and parallels, which should have respect to all varieties of things, as stars, plants, minerals, which are extant in the great world." [14] But Bacon's sturdy common sense and his practical and prosaic mind are no sure guides to the most characteristic ways of thinking of his generation. Paracelsus had gone to bombastic extremes, yet he was no more obsessed with the mystical interrelationships of the universe than was the gentle German philosopher, Jacob Boehme, whose work affected poets, philosophers, artists, and scientists. "Man is the great mystery of God," he wrote, "the Microcosm, or the complete abridgement of the Universe." [15] The essence of his teaching was perhaps contained in one sentence: "All is in Man, both Heaven and Earth, Stars and Planets; and also the Number Three of the Deity." Burton lamented the Fall of man all the more because man was created "Microcosmus, a little world, a modell of the World, Soveraigne Lord of the Earth, Viceroy of the World, sole Commander and Governour of all the creatures in it." [16] God said, declared Philip Stubbes, *"Faciamus Hominem,* let us make Man; that is, a

---

[13] Benesch, *Art of the Renaissance,* pp. 47–51.
[14] *Advancement of Learning,* IV.ii.
[15] *Signatura Rerum, or the Signatures of all Things,* trans. by J. Ellinstone (London, 1651).
[16] *Anatomy of Melancholy,* p. 1.

wonderful Creature; and therefore is called in Greek MICRO-COSMOS, a little world in himself." [17] Donne went farther: "The Philosopher draws man into too narrow a table, when he says he is the *Microcosmos*, an Abridgement of the world in little." Rather, man is *"Mundum Magnum*, a world to which all the rest of the world is but subordinate." [18]

If this was metaphor, it was certainly the most pervasive figure of the late Renaissance in England, "a conceit," wrote a forgotten writer, "as dear to some Ancient and Modern Writers as their very eyes." There was a time when Sir Thomas Browne had so dismissed it, but as he pondered he came to believe that it was mystical, metaphysical, even scientific truth. He wrote in the *Religio Medici:* "That we are the breath and similitude of God, it is indisputable, and upon record of Holy Scripture; but to call ourselves a Microcosm, or little World, I thought it onely a pleasant trope of Rhetorick, till my neer judgement and second thoughts told me there was a real truth therein." The "truth" of which he became aware was that man was a "little world" in that he contained in himself every gradation of life, from the lowest to the highest:

For first we are a rude mass, and in the rank of creatures which onely are, and have a dull kind of being, not yet priviledged with life, or preferred to sense or reason; next we live the life of Plants, the life of Animals, the life of Men, and at last the life of Spirits, running on in one mysterious nature those five kinds of existences, which comprehend the creatures, not onely of the World, but of the Universe.

"Thus is man," Browne concluded in one of his most characteristic and most familiar passages, "that great and true *Am-*

[17] *Anatomie of Abuses*, ed. by F. G. Furnivall (London, 1877–79), p. iii.
[18] Sermon xxv, *XXVI Sermons* (London, 1661).

phibium, whose nature is disposed to live, not onely like other creatures in divers elements, but in divided and distinguished worlds." [19] From this time forth, the term microcosm is often on his lips: "Whilst I study to find how I am a Microcosm, or little World, I find my self something more than the great." "That truest Microcosm, the Womb of our Mother . . ." "There is no man alone, because every man is a Microcosm, and carries the whole World about him." "The World that I regard is my self; it is the Microcosm of my frame that I cast mine eyes on; for the other I use it but like my Globe, and turn it round sometimes for my recreation." In the *Garden of Cyrus,* Browne was almost as much obsessed with the repetition of the macrocosm in the microcosm as Paracelsus had been with that "Homunculus," or little man, he boasted he could create in a laboratory limbeck.

True amphibia as they were, our seventeenth-century ancestors became more poignantly aware of the interlockings of macrocosm, geocosm, and microcosm at the moment when the advancement of learning was breaking down old ideas of the universe, the world, and man, beginning to replace them with something much more "modern"—if less beautiful. Any of them might have said of man:

> Thou art a world, thy self alone,
> Yea, three great worlds refin'd to one. [20]

II

Shakespeare, I have suggested, was probably less conscious of three worlds than Donne became even during Shakespeare's lifetime. The Elizabethans used the word macrocosm broadly: it might indicate the whole of things—the universe,

---

[19] *Religio Medici,* I.xxxiv.   [20] Vaughan, *The Character: to Etesia.*

including the earth; on occasion it might mean the world or earth, as distinguished from man. However as the Renaissance mind was becoming more aware of earth, thanks to exploration and discovery, and more aware of the universe, thanks to Copernicus and Tycho Brahe, the term macrocosm became more significant and more complex. It will make my problem easier if from the beginning I make a distinction between the three worlds, by adding another word to our vocabulary. Let us use "macrocosm" for the universe; "microcosm" for man, and "geocosm" for the terrestrial globe, as distinguished from both the universe and man. Before we are ready to understand some of the correspondences which were read into "the little world of man," let us see how man thought of both macrocosm and geocosm.

"God himself," said Donne in one of his Platonic sermons, "made all he made according to a pattern. God had deposited and laid up in himself certain forms, patterns, Ideas of everything that he made. He made nothing of which he had not preconceived the form." [21] The pattern of the old Ptolemaic universe was simple and readily intelligible. "This is Nature's nest of Boxes," as Donne said. "The Heavens containe the Earth, the Earth cities, Cities Men. And all these are concentrique." The outermost circle of the fixed stars included, in nice gradation, the perfect spheres of each of the planets; the innermost circle was the sphere of the earth. Such at least had been the state of things at the time of Creation. Later, according to many theologians, the sphere of earth included within itself the last and most ominous circle of all—Hell, embodied in the exact center of earth.

The basic principles of the original Creation had been *harmony* and *proportion*, words that persistently echo in the

[21] "Sermon to the King, April 1628."

ethics and aesthetics of the Renaissance. "All things began in Order; so shall they end, according to the Ordainer of Order and the mystical Mathematicks of the City of Heaven."

> From harmony, from heavenly harmony,
> This universal frame began.

At the Creation the morning stars sang together while all the sons of God shouted with joy. The old idea of the music of the spheres was easily adapted to the "saintly shout and solemn jubily" of seraphim and cherubim, singing to celestial accompaniment in those days before

> disproportioned sin
> Jarred against nature's chime, and with harsh din
> Broke the fair music that all creatures made
> To their great Lord, whose love their motion swayed
> In perfect diapason,   (*At a Solemn Music*)

For centuries poets had used such musical figures as Lorenzo's to describe the harmony of the universe.

> Look, how the floor of heaven
> Is thick inlaid with patines of bright gold;
> There's not the smallest orb which thou beholdst
> But in his motion like an angel sings,
> Still quiring to the young-eyed cherubins,—
> Such harmony is in immortal souls.
>   (*Merchant of Venice*, v.i.58–63)

"God made the whole world," wrote Donne, "in such an uniformity, such a concinnity of parts, as that it was an Instrument, perfectly in tune."[22] Long after astronomy had given the final blow to belief in the music of the spheres, poets were still adapting the ancient idea. "There is a music,"

[22] *Sermons*, ed. by L. P. Smith (Oxford, 1920), p. 162.

as Sir Thomas Browne said, "where ever there is a harmony, order, or proportion; and thus far we may maintain the music of the Sphears; for those well-ordered motions, and regular paces, though they give no sound unto the air, yet to the understanding they strike a note most full of harmony." [23] Addison was perhaps versifying Browne when he concluded *The Spacious Firmament on High:*

> What though in solemn silence all
> Move round the dark terrestrial ball;
> What though nor real voice nor sound
> Amidst their radiant orbs be found?
> In Reason's ear they all rejoice,
> And utter forth a glorious voice;
> For ever singing as they shine,
> "The Hand that made us is divine."

Even if the spheres no longer sang together, they still maintained a stately cosmic dance:

> The Sphaeres have Musick, but they have no tongue,
> Their harmony is rather danc'd than sung. [24]

Sir John Davies in his elaborate symphony *Orchestra* described the original cosmic dance of elements and planets:

> Dancing, bright Lady, then began to be,
> When the first seeds, whereof the world did spring,
> The fire, air, earth, and water did agree,
> By Love's persuasion, nature's mighty king,
> To leave their first disorder'd combating,
>   And in a dance such measure to observe
>   As all the world their motion should preserve.

[23] *Religio Medici,* II.ix.
[24] Donne, *Upon the Translation of the Psalms by Sir Philip Sidney.*

> Since when they still are carried, in a round,
> And changing, come one in another's place;
> Yet doe they neither mingle nor confound,
> But every one doth keepe the bounded space.[25]

Davies's universe was still Ptolemaic; his "earth doth stand for ever still." But the cosmic dance was even more splendid when adapted to a Copernican universe, in which the central sun was the symbol of God,

> Whose brightnesse passeth every creatures sight.
> Yet round about him stird with gentle fire
> All things do dance; their being, action, might,
> They thither do direct with strong desire,
> To embosome him with close embracements they aspire.

> Unseen, incomprehensible, He moves
> About himself each seeking entity
> That never yet shall find that which it loves:
> No finite thing can reach infinity,
> No thing dispers'd comprehend that Unity,
> Yet in their ranks they seemly foot it round,
> Trip it with joy at the worlds harmony,
> Struck with the pleasure of an amorous stound,
> So dance they with fair flowers from unknown root
> ycrownd [26]

As all things were created in harmony, so they were created in proportion. So far as the macrocosm was concerned, symmetry was clearly displayed in the old Ptolemaic spheres, but we shall better understand the principle of proportion if we turn from the macrocosm to the more comprehensible geocosm. Like the universe, the globe of earth was created

---

[25] Sir John Davies, *Orchestra*, stanzas 17–18. Cf. Gretchen Finney, "A World of Instruments," *E.L.H.*, XX (1953), 87–120.

[26] Henry More, *Psychathanasia*, III.iii.12.

circular in form. There were those, indeed, who insisted that at the Creation the earth had been a complete sphere, with no mountains and no depths to mar its circular perfection. But the more usual conception was that with which we are familiar—that, when God separated the land from the water, the earth emerged in the general form in which we know it. "I would examine that demonstration of Alexander Picolomineus," said Burton in one of the many passages in which he pondered the state of the original earth, "whether the earth's superficies be bigger than the sea's." For centuries the Church Fathers had debated that question, many insisting that the Geometer who laid the measures must have drawn his original plan of the world in exact proportion so far as land and water were concerned. Since God's line had gone forth throughout the world, symmetry must be everywhere. Working originally with equal areas of land and sea, Deity on the third day had hollowed out the land in order to form beds for the waters. The land was piled upon the remainder of the earth, forming mountains and hills; the bed of sea then corresponded exactly to the bed of land, in its turn exhibiting valleys, channels, abysses. Milton's Angel, who had been present at the Creation, described the original "proportions" of earth to Adam:

> Immediately the mountains huge appear
> Emergent, and their broad bare backs upheave
> Into the clouds; their tops ascend the sky.
> So high as heaved the tumid hills, so low
> Down sunk a hollow bottom broad and deep,
> Capacious bed of waters.   (*PL*, VII.285–91)

For every mountain that had been exalted, a plain had been hollowed into a valley or abyss. "Hast thou entered into the springs of the sea? or hast thou walked in the search of the deep?" asked the Voice of God. No one had done so, yet there were many Renaissance men who believed, as had their fathers before them, that if man could actually walk in the search of the deep, he would find exact duplication, valley for hill, abyss for mountain.

These were far from being the only "proportions" of the original earth, for symmetry existed everywhere, as we shall find. But these basic ideas of the creation of both macrocosm and geocosm may serve for the present to explain the constant stress we find upon "harmony," "symmetry," and "proportion" in the universe and in man, and serve too to explain a persistent idea, never more succinctly expressed than by George Herbert in *Man:*

> Man is all symmetrie,
> Full of proportions, one limbe to another,
> And all to all the world besides:
> Each part may call the furthest, brother:
> For head with foot hath private amitie,
> And both with moons and tides.

III

For all their interest in the other worlds, the early seventeenth-century poets were most interested in the little world of man, if we may trust the evidence of both serious and frivolous prose and poetry. They could have their fun with the microcosmic figure, as did William Hammond when he wrote of his grey hair turning white:

> I shall a perfect microcosm grow
> When, as the Alps, I crowned am with snow.

> I will believe this white the milky way
> Which leads into the endless court of May.[27]

They could use it for a spectacle. Ben Jonson's *Masque of Hymen* introduced "a masque of eight men" issuing "out of a microcosm or globe figuring man." The immense popularity of the idea is suggested by the many titles of both serious and light books, of which these are only a sampling: *Micro-cosmo-graphia: The Little Worlds Description, or the Map of Man; Microcosmographia: A Description of the Body of Man; Microcosmographia, or a Piece of the World Discovered in Essays and Characters; Microcosmos, The Discovery of the Little World, with the Government Thereof; The Wonders of the Little World; Wits Theater of the Little World.*[28] There was occasional laughter, but on the whole the treatment of the microcosm was serious.

Wherever we look, we find a profusion of epithets and synonyms for the microcosm: "the Little World, wherein the Great is shown"; "this little kingdom man"; "the truest Mappe of the World, a summarie and compendious other World"; "the mirrour of nature"; "the quintessence extract'd from the Macrocosm." Piling Pelion on Ossa, Burton spoke in the *Anatomy* of "Man, the most excellent, and noble creature of the World, *the principall and mighty worke of God, wonder of Nature,* as Zoroastes calls him; *audacis naturae miraculum, the marvaile of marvailes,* as Plato; *the Abridge-*

[27] *Welcome, Grey Hairs,* in *Minor Poets of the Caroline Period,* II, 509.

[28] Henry Smith, *Micro-cosmo-graphia,* trans. by Joshuah Sylvester, in *Complete Works of Sylvester,* ed. by Alexander Grosart (Edinburgh, 1880); Helkin Crooke, *Microcosmographia: A Description of the Body of Man* (London, 1616); John Earle, *Microcosmographia: or a Piece of the World Discovered in Essays and Characters* (London, 1628); Peter Heyln, *Microcosmos: A Little Description of the Great World* (Oxford, 1616); Nathaniel Wanley, *The Wonders of the Little World, Or a General History of Man in Six Books* (London, 1678); Robert Allott, *Wits Theater of the Little World* (London, 1599).

ment and Epitome of the World, as Pliny; *Microcosmos*, a
little World."[29] Man was not only an epitome of earth; he
was a little copy of God:

> For what had all this All, which Man in one
> Did not unite; the earth, aire, water, fire,
> Life, sense, and spirit, nay, the powrefull throne
> Of the divinest Essence, did retire,
> And his owne Image into Clay inspire:
> > So that this Creature well might called be
> > Of the great world, the small epitome,
> Of the dead world, the live, and quicke anatomie.[30]

If it was true that man was not only a copy of God but a
"Mappe" of the world and an "Epitome" of the universe—
and there were few who did not so believe at the beginning
of the seventeenth century—it was no wonder that men
studied that "Mappe" as closely as they pored upon geographical globes in their studies, and followed new discoveries
in anatomy as in astronomy, seeking in themselves a clue to
the riddles of the universe. Bewildered by the ever increasing complexity of Nature, seventeenth-century man sought a
key to the unity which he felt sure must exist among the
three worlds, and for many years he continued to find it, as
had his medieval ancestors, in what he called "correspondences" between macrocosm, geocosm, and microcosm. Correspondences had long been of many sorts. Perhaps the sim-
plest was the recurrence of numbers. "I have often admired
the mystical way of Pythagoras," said Browne, "and the secret
magic of numbers." Were there not seven planets, seven
notes in the harmony of the spheres, seven days of Creation,
seven ages of the world? Inevitably there were seven ages of

[29] *Anatomy of Melancholy*, I.i, Mem. 1, p. 1.
[30] Giles Fletcher, *Christs Victorie in Heaven*, in *Poetical Works*, I, 20.

man, seven virtues, seven deadly sins, seven wonders of the world, seven sages, even seven gates of Thebes. If one preferred the mystic number five, he might find quincunxes in heaven and earth, as did Browne. Donne could use the analogy to tease or flatter the ladies, as he did in *The Primrose:*

> Live Primrose then, and thrive
> With thy true number five;
> And women, whom this flower doth represent,
> With this mysterious number, be content;
> Ten is the farthest number; if halfe ten
> Belonge unto each woman, then
> Each woman may take halfe us men;
> Or if this will not serve their turne, Since all
> Numbers are odde or even, and they fall
> First into this, five, women may take us all.

Kepler himself described his ecstasy over the planetary relationships of the five regular solids. And Newton used as one proof of his theories of color and sound correspondences between the prismatic colors and the musical scale. Mystic numbers were not only the stuff of poetry for metaphysical wits; scientists could find them in the intricate repetitions of an expert Craftsman, who had set his riddles fairly that all who would read might understand the essential relationship of macrocosm and microcosm.

Indeed the Deity of this period often seemed a metaphysical wit delighting in puzzles. Browne found the meaning of the universe in his five-sided quincunx; Donne, in his early religious fervor, saw the symbol of the cross repeated everywhere in nature:

> Since Christ embrac'd the Crosse it selfe, dare I
> His image, th' image of his Crosse deny? . . .
> Who can deny mee power, and liberty

> To stretch mine armes, and mine owne Crosse to be?
> Swimme, and at every stroake, thou art thy Crosse;
> The mast and yard make one, where seas do tosse;
> Looke downe, thou spiest out Crosses in small things;
> Looke up, thou seest birds rais'd on crossed wings;
> All the Globes frame, and spheares, is nothing else
> But the Meridians crossing Parallels.   (*The Crosse*)

As widespread as belief in numerology and patterns was that in "signatures."

> Who hath the vertue to expresse the rare
> And curious vertues both of herbs and stones?

Herbert asked in *Providence*, in which he set down many of the homely lessons of the Galenic herbalists, indicating how imbalance of the humors might be corrected:

> Most herbs that grow in brooks are hot and dry.
> Cold fruits warm kernells help against the winde.
> The lemmons juice and rinde cure mutually,
> The whey of milk doth loose, the mild doth binde.

"A rose besides his beauty is a cure," he wrote, and said again, "Herbs gladly cure our flesh because that they / Finde their acquaintance there." The emblem books of the seventeenth century, like the bestiaries of the Middle Ages, emphasized similarities between man and minerals, metals, plants, animals.

> Goe, and catche a falling starre,
>   Get with child a mandrake roote,
> Tell me, where all past yeares are,
>   Or who cleft the Divels foot,

wrote John Donne, who could dismiss the old superstition of the mandrake root with other "vulgar errors," though he himself believed many another superstition. Many of his contemporaries still accepted the old legend of the mandrake, the root of which bore a striking similarity to the nude human form. Far down into the century men as learned as Donne accepted the doctrine of signatures. Sir Thomas Browne wrote: "I hold moreover that here is a Phytognomy, or Physiognomy, not only of Men, but of Plants and Vegetables; and in every one of them some outward figures which hang as signs or bushes of their inward forms. The Finger of God hath left an inscription upon all his works, not graphical or composed of Letters, but of their several forms, constitutions, parts and operations, which, aptly joyned together, do make one word that doth express their natures. By these Letters God called the Stars by their names; and by this Alphabet Adam assigned to every creature a name peculiar to its Nature." [31] A still more learned philosopher, Henry More, the Cambridge Platonist, used the "signatures" of plants as one of his important proofs that everywhere in the universe man might find evidence of the power and providence of God. Such signatures, he declared, are "like the Inscriptions upon Apothecaries Boxes, that the Master of the Shop sets on that the Apprentice may read them; nay, it is better for here is in Herbs described the very nature and use of them, not the mere name." Perhaps the cures accepted by Henry More do not appear in the British Pharmacopoeia, but they were not very different from cures used by our grandmothers, which more than once proved efficacious; Quinces, said More, are a downy and hairy fruit; what more logical than that a "decoction of Quinces" should prove "good for the fetching again Hair that has fallen"? Scorpion-grass, formed like the crooked tail of a scorpion, should prove spe-

[31] *Religio Medici*, II.ii.

cific against the bites of poisonous insects. Adder's-tongue, and indeed all speckled plants with spots like the spotted skin of snakes, were antidotes for snake bite and soothing in the case of stings. "Wall-nuts bear the whole signature of the Head. The outward green Cortex answers to the Pericranium, and a salt made of it is singularly good for wounds in that part; as the kernel is good for the Brains, which it resembles." More proved his point logically, if not physiologically, for surely it would be difficult to find a better "epitome" for the human head than in More's walnut. "Thus," the Cambridge Platonist seriously concluded a long section of his most important work, "did Divine Providence by natural Hieroglyphicks read short Physick Lectures to the rude wit of man." [32]

If God had imprinted signatures upon planets and stones, how much more likely that He had placed His stamp upon His copy, man. "There are mystically in our faces certain Characters which carry in them the motto of our Souls, wherein he that cannot read A.B.C. may read our natures," said Browne. His curious mind went on to ponder not only "the common wonder of all men, how among so many millions of faces, there should be none alike," but even more the significance of markings in the human hand, no two of which (he discovered long before Bertillon) were alike. Surely this extraordinary example of diversity in apparent unity had been meant as a clue to man: the "mystical figures in our Hands," Browne said, "I dare not call meer dashes, strokes *à la volée,* or at random, because delineated by a Pencil that never works in vain." [33] But God's stamp had not been limited to hands and faces. "Thou hast not thy beginning from the fecundity, power, nor action of the elemental qualities, being an imme-

---

[32] *Antidote against Atheism* II.vi (London, 1642).
[33] *Religio Medici,* II.ii.

diate masterpiece of that great Maker," wrote Jacob Boehme
in *Signatura Rerum;* "hence hast thou the forms and figures
of all things imprinted in thee from thy first original."

Both the world and the universe were repeated in the structure of man's body. In his "round head," a copy of the
sphere of the universe, man might find the whole cosmic system, written in small with mystical meaning:

> This little worlds two little starres are eyes;
> And he that all eyes framed, fram'd all others
> Downward to fall, but these to clime the skies,
> There to acquaint them with their starrie brothers;
>> Planets fixt in the head (this spheare of sense)
>> Yet wandring still through heaven's circumference,
>> The Intellect being their Intelligence.[34]

But it was still easier to find correspondences in man's body
for the geocosm. Never did the ingenuity of allegorizing
poets carry such similarities further than did Phineas Fletcher
in *The Purple Island,* over which I pause, both because it is
the most extreme example in verse of the geocosm-microcosm
analogy, and because it will later show us how geology and
physiology were retarded by the attempt of man to interpret
the world in his own image. In *The Purple Island* Fletcher
racked his brains and exhausted his sources—as he exhausts
his readers—to find analogies in the geocosm for every part
of man's body, external and internal. From the beginning
of the poem we hear not only double- but triple-talk: we
think now of the earth, again of man, sometimes of this
"blessed Isle, this England," for the "Purple Island" is all
three. Fletcher begins with the Creation: on the third day,
a world emerged from the waters, a great island in a bound-

<hr>

[34] Phineas Fletcher, *Upon the Contemplation of the B. of Excester,* in
Works, II, 247.

less sea; on the last day of Creation, God brought forth another isle within this island:

> Now when the first weeks life was almost spent,
>   And this world built, and richly furnish'd; . . .
> He cast to frame an Isle, the heart and head
>   Of all his works, compos'd with curious art;
>   Which like an Index briefly should impart
> The summe of all; the whole, yet of the whole a part. (1.43)

> Look as a scholar, who doth closely gather
> Many large volumes in a narrow place;
> So that great Wisdome all this All together
> Confin'd into this Islands little space;
>   And being one, soon into two he fram'd it;
>   And now made two, to one again reclaim'd it;
> The little *Isle of Man,* or *Purple Island* nam'd it.   (1.48)

It is a rocky isle that "grounded lies upon a sure foundation, / Compact and hard"; here we have the bones of the world and the bones of the body, covered with "fat earth," surrounded for protection by skin, "that round spreading fence, / Which like a sea girts th' Isle in every part." A little kingdom, the isle is divided into three parts, jointly "sway'd by three Metropolies." In the copious marginal glosses, which sometimes clarify and often confuse his allegories, Fletcher has indicated, much more briefly than in his involved verses, the three regions of the Isle of Man: "the lowest, or belly; the middle, or breast; the highest, or head." For every organ, every bone, every function of the several parts of each "Metropolie" he found exact correspondence in the geocosm. An elaborate "anatomy," written in an age that delighted in anatomies of man, of the world, of melancholy, *The Purple Island* lays open the bodies of both man and the world, studying the intricate structure and the processes. Skin, flesh, cartilage, ligament, muscles, nerves, sinews, stomach, bladder, liver, spleen—they are all here, together with their corre- spondences in the globe. The heart is the governing city, the head a tower, the liver a well, the kidneys twin moun- tains, and the stomach, it would seem, a communal kitchen:

> Below dwells in this Cities market-place
> The Islands common Cook, Concoction;
> Common to all; therefore in middle space
> Is quarter'd fit in just proportion . . .
>
> That heat, which in his furnace ever fumeth,
> Is nothing like to our hot parching fire;
> Which all consuming, self at length consumeth;
> But moistning flames a gentle heat inspire.   (II.33–34)

A little of *The Purple Island* goes a very long way, and I do not pretend to have mastered all the intricacies of its twelve cantoes and seven hundred stanzas. As poetry, *The Purple Island* is negligible; as a handbook of Elizabethan physiology, it has its historical interest; as a handbook of geology, it remains a warning of the dangers faced by men who, knowing little of the structure of either, read analogies from man's body into the earth and read them back again.

Yet Fletcher was merely versifying ideas widely current in his day. If his physiology and his geology were already somewhat antiquated, his method was not. We shall see that the macrocosm-microcosm analogy remained for many years to dominate the minds of various important scientists who continued to discover the processes of one world in another.

IV

One further theme remains before we shall be ready to think as our ancestors thought and—I hope—better understand the metaphors of Elizabethan and seventeenth-century poets. We have seen the extent to which the three worlds were interlocked and interrelated by the repetition of the phenomena of one in another. We have become aware, through persistent analogies, that the correspondence between man and his world was even closer than between man and his universe, because he knew his world better than he knew his universe and it was more comprehensible to men whose immediate ancestors had discovered so much of it. As man and the world were created in time, so also they had their periods: seven ages of man, seven ages of the world. There was no heresy more hotly denied by the medieval Fathers and the orthodox of the Renaissance than a heresy of Aristotle —that the world is eternal. The world had its birth and growth; it was also subject to decay and dissolution. It would continue its course only

> till that day come
> Which shall the earth to cinders doom,
> And a fierce feaver must calcine
> The body of this world like thine,
> My Little World! [35]

"O ruin'd piece of nature!" reflected Gloucester, as Lear shrank from his own hand that smelt of mortality, "This great world / Shall so wear out to naught."

> Me seemes the world is runne quite out of square
> From the first point of his appointed course,
> And being once amisse, growes daily wourse and wourse,

lamented Spenser in the *Faerie Queene*.[36] "I am fallen into a cold sweate," wrote Godfrey Goodman, one of the chief apos-

[35] Henry King, *The Exequy*, in *Minor Poets of the Caroline Period*, III, 196.
[36] Book V, Prologue, stanza 1.

tles of the world's decay, "and am suddenly stroken with great
feare and confusion . . . for when I observe the course of
things, the severall actions and inclinations of men; when I
consider the diseases of these times, together with all the
signes, tokens, and symptomes; alas, alas, I feare a relapse, I
feare a relapse, lest the world in her doting old age, should
not againe turne infidell, and that the end of us be worse than
the beginning." [37] At the end of the sixteenth century man
was closer than ever to the end of the world, and the chorus
of despondency and despair over the approaching death of
the world grew daily more profound. The world "doeth
waxe old and every part thereof doeth feele some debilitie
and weaknesse." The death of Elizabeth in age in 1603, the
death of Prince Henry in youth in 1612 were preludes to
outpourings of the approaching disaster.

> Our Sinnes have so the Elements defil'd
>   That they with Fire must needed refined be:
> Nay, more; our sins the Heav'ns themselves have soil'd;
>   Then melt they must, from soile to set them free.[38]

So the melancholy chorus continued: man decays and the
earth decays, and the end is dissolution or destruction. As
late as 1664, long after the premises of the argument for decay of the world had been undermined, Henry Power, one
of the chief prophets of optimism, told of "The Universal
Exclamation of the World's decay and approximation to its
period; That both the great and little World have long since
pass'd the Meridian, and, That the Faculties of the one doe
fade and decay, as well as the Fabricks and Materials of the

---

[37] *Fall of Man* (1616), pp. 2–3; quoted in Victor Harris, *All Coherence
Gone* (Chicago, 1949), p. 41.
[38] John Davies of Hereford, *The Muses Sacrifice*, in *The Complete
Works*, ed. by A. B. Grosart (London, 1878), p. 50.

other; which though it be a Conceit that hath possess'd all ages past, as nearly as ours, yet the Clamour was never so high as it is now." [39]

There was little possibility of any other way of thinking, so long as the geocosm-microcosm analogy maintained its hold upon the imagination of men, who, conscious of their own mortality, read decay into the earth of which they were an inextricable part. Little by little the discoveries of science were undermining the basis of that analogy. The Century of Revolutions saw no revolution greater than that rightabout-face which occurred in human thinking after man discovered the real nature of a universe, a world, and a body that had long remained mysteries. The clear light of reason of the Restoration, which dispelled many shadows, put an end to a way of thinking held for hundreds of years by men who dwelt in three closely related worlds, an integral part of each of them. It left science richer, but poetry poorer.

Whatever the effect of science—of that we shall hear more—perhaps the literary death-blow to the microcosm was given by that son of the Enlightenment, Jonathan Swift. *A Tale of a Tub* is the greatest parody of its time, in which Olympian laughter was turned against the whole seventeenth century: its styles, its manners, its religion, its learning, its science, its enthusiasms. Embedded in the tale of the three brothers is a satiric epitome of all we have been reading here. Peter, Martin, and Jack had inherited from their father the new coats that were his only heritage to them—coats that still carry on the old figure, since they were to "grow in the same proportion as your bodies, lengthening and widening of themselves, so as to be always fit." From their simple home they went up to town, where they discovered a sect "whose

[39] Henry Power, *Experimental Philosophy* (London, 1664), p. 188.

tenets obtained and spread very far, especially in the *grande monde*, and among everybody of good fashion." The chief tenet of the sect's belief was an elaborate parody of the macrocosm and microcosm:

They held the universe to be a large suit of clothes which invests everything; that the earth is invested by air; the air is invested by the stars; and the stars are invested by the *Primum Mobile*. Look on this globe of earth, you will find it to be a very complete and fashionable dress. What is that which some call land but a fine coat faced with green, or the sea but a waistcoat of water-tabby? Proceed to the particular works of the creation, you will find how curious journeyman Nature hath been to trim up the vegetable beaux; observe how sparkish a periwig adorns the head of a beech, and what a fine doublet of white satin is worn by the birch. To conclude from all, what is man himself but a micro-coat, or rather a complete suit of clothes with all its trimmings?

Swift satirically dismissed the tropes and figures of the microcosmists as mere decorations upon the micro-coat: "embroidery was sheer wit, . . . gold lace was repartee. . . . All of which required abundance of finesse and delicatesse to manage with advantage, as well as a strict observance after times and fashions." As the age wore on, embroidery and gold lace came to adorn the poetry of the microcosmists, and the "conceit" of witty simile took the place of what had been "image," revealing truth. With the macrocosm and the microcosm something disappeared from literature. George Herbert wrote the epitaph of the most charming poetry our language has ever known:

> Farewell, sweet phrases, lovely metaphors, . . .
> Lovely enchanting language, sugar-cane,
> Hony of roses, whither wilt thou flie?

2

THE CIRCLE OF PERFECTION

"One of the most convenient Hieroglyphicks of God is a circle," Donne wrote in his *Devotions*, "and a circle is endlesse; His Sun and Moone and Stars move circularly." More completely than in any other symbol in the universe, the Great Geometer had shown the intricate relationship of the three worlds in the repetition of the Circle of Perfection, which He alone transcended, since, as Pascal, Browne and a dozen others said, echoing an ancient phrase: "God is a Circle, whose Circumference is nowhere and whose Centre everywhere." No metaphor was more loved by Renaissance poets than that of the circle, which they had inherited from Pythagorean and Platonic ancestors, who in turn had borrowed it from orientals, to whom the serpent, swallowing its tail, was an "Hieroglyphick" of eternity,

> because in your vast mouth you hold your Tayle,
> As coupling Ages past with times to come.[1]

[1] Fulke Greville, "Eternitie." Cf. Marston's *Histriomastix*, in which a "Teacher" explains time to a student:

> this time
> Wee call a yeere; whose Hierocliptick was
> (Amongst the Egyptians) figured in a Snake
> Wreath'd circular, the tayle within his mouth:

"Time swallows all that's past and more," wrote a forgotten poet of the seventeenth century, "yet time is swallow'd in eternity."

The circle implied both the beginning and the end of all created things. "Of this Figure," Sir Thomas Browne wrote in the *Garden of Cyrus*, "Plato made choice to illustrate the motion of the soul, both of the world and man; while he delivereth that God divided the whole conjunction length-wise, according to the figure of a Greek X, and then turning it about reflected it into a circle; By the circle implying the uniform motion of the first Orb, and by the right line, the planetical and various motions within it." Indeed, for all its quincunxes, Browne's *Garden of Cyrus* was, in part, a disquisition on the circle, since his quincunx, like Plato's five regular solids, could be inscribed in a sphere. "The number of five," as he said, "is remarkable in every Circle, not only as the first sphaerical Number, but the measure of sphaerical motion. For sphaerical bodies move by fives." As the circle signified the beginning, so it prophesied the end. If the Greek *chi* reminded man of the divine origin of the soul, another Greek character, *theta* Θ—a combination of circle and straight lines, and the first letter of *Thanatos*, or Death—was his evidence of mortality. "Circles and right lines," as Browne said, "limit and close up all besides, and the mortall right-lined circle must conclude and shut up all." [2] God's symbol was the circle, man's the straight line. We shall see how this emphasis changed as time went on, but for the present we are among a generation of poets who still saw the Circle of Perfection in

---

As (happily) the Latines (since) did call
A Ring (of the word *Annus*) *Annulus*.

[2] *Garden of Cyrus*, III–IV; *Hydriotaphia*, v (Keynes ed., IV, 117, 95; IV, 45).

the universe, in the globe, in the little world of man, and read it into their metaphysics, their ethics, their aesthetics, and their theories of cosmic and of human history.

"Placed on this isthmus of a middle state," between the incomprehensible great and the equally incomprehensible small, Pascal in his *Thoughts* saw the circle in both macrocosm and microcosm, as he turned from the vast circle of the sun, "that brilliant light, set like an eternal lamp to illumine the universe," to "another prodigy equally astonishing," the body of man with "veins in the limbs, blood in the veins, humours in the blood, drops in the humours." Always he was conscious of the *Sphaera cujus centrum ubique, circumferentia nullibi,* of which Browne said, "That allegorical description of Hermes pleaseth me beyond all the Metaphysical definitions of Divines." [3] The center and the circumference of the circle are persistent symbols among seevnteenth-century writers for God, for the world, and for man. Before the new astronomy changed the place of the world, earth was the center, the heavens the circumference; but whatever the location of his world, man was, as he has always remained, a center to that he sought to comprehend. Seeking God in a new universe that had grown beyond comprehension, the religious poets sometimes thought Him lost, as did Herbert momentarily in *The Search:*

> My knees pierce the earth, mine eyes the skie,
> > And yet the sphere
> And centre both denie
> > That thou art there.

In one of his emblem-poems Quarles applied the figure less to the universe than to a chaotic world:

[3] Marginal gloss, *Religio Medici,* I.x (Keynes ed., I, 14).

> The world's a seeming paradise, but her own
>   And man's tormentor;
> Appearing fix'd, yet but a rolling stone
>   Without a tenter;
> It is a vast circumference, where none
>   Can find a centre.   (*Emblems,* i.vi)

Donne in his tortuous lines on the death of Prince Henry was concerned rather with man's center than with God's:

> Looke to mee faith, and looke to my faith, God;
> For both my centers feele this period.
> Of waight one center, one of greatnesse is;
> And Reason is that center, Faith is this;
> For into our reason flow, and there do end
> All, that this naturall world doth comprehend:
> Quotidian things, and equidistant hence,
> Shut in, for man, in one circumference.

God might transcend the circle, but He had created the soul of man to love the circle of the universe, as Plotinus suggested: "The Soul is ceaselessly leading the Cosmos towards itself; the continuous attraction communicates a continuous movement . . . in the curving course in which the moving body at every stage possesses the Soul that is attracting it and bestowing itself upon it. . . . The Soul exists in revolution around God to whom it clings in love, holding itself to the utmost of its power near to Him as the Being on which all depends." [4] For centuries the accepted Ptolemaic astronomy had been man's supreme proof that the universe, like the world and the soul of man, was spherical. From the *primum mobile* to the round earth, one sphere nestled into another, the whole an elaborate yet readily comprehensible series of circles within circles all designed for man, who lived at the

[4] *Enneads,* VII.ix.8–9, trans. by Stephen McKenna (5 vols.; London, 1917–30).

center upon the innermost sphere of all. At the Creation, when God had imposed order upon chaos and bade the sun and moon and planets to take their places in the celestial hierarchy, the heavenly bodies began to move in the circular form:

> Hark! In what rings
> And hymning circulations, the quick world
> Awakes and sings! . . .
> Thus all is hurl'd
> In sacred Hymns and Order, The great Chime
> And symphony of nature.[5]

Like Sir John Davies in *Orchestra*, Milton took for granted that the circular motion was native to the elements:

> Air, and ye Elements, the eldest birth
> Of Nature's womb, that in quaternion run
> Perpetual circle.   *(PL,* v.180–82)

Less obsessed with the Circle of Perfection than were many of his earlier contemporaries, Milton nevertheless, like Dante, read it into heaven. On that solemn day when "by imperial summons called," the innumerable host of heaven thronged to God's throne to hear his pronouncement, "This day I have begot whom I declare My only Son," the angels stood "in orbs of circuit inexpressible. . . . Orb within Orb." The announcement made, the angels, like the planets, celebrated in cosmic dance:

> That day, as other solemn days, they spent
> In song and dance about the sacred hill—
> Mystical dance, which yonder starry sphere
> Of planets and of fixed in all her wheels
> Resembles nearest; mazes intricate,

[5] Vaughan, *The Morning Watch.*

Eccentric, intervolved, yet regular
Then most when most irregular they seem;
And in their motions harmony divine
So smooths her charming tones that God's own ear
Listens delighted.   (*PL,* v.618–27)

Their dance ended, the angels still maintained their cosmic pattern:

Forthwith from dance to sweet repast they turn
Desirous; all in circles as they stood,
Tables are set.   (*PL,* v.630–32)

The God of the earlier seventeenth century was a "skillful Geometrician" whose nature was to express Himself mathematically. While He might "with one stroak of his Compass" have described or divided a line, He preferred the Circle of Perfection to the Right Line of Mortality. Milton, never more reverent than when he dealt with scenes of the Creation, described the Son creating a world with geometric compasses.

Like the geocosm, the microcosmic body of man repeated the circle. Phineas Fletcher's third and "highest precinct," man's head,

the best and chief of all,
Though least in compasse, and of narrow space,
Was therefore fram'd like heaven, sphericall,
Of largest figure, and of loveliest grace.

Indeed the surrealists of that day—who were the poets as well as the painters—drew their pictures of the human body not in a succession of cubes but in circles and cylinders, parabolas, arcs, and ellipses, striving—in the words of a seventeenth-century writer—for "that perfection which is found in the Spherical Figure, which God hath also pourtray'd in all his works, which observe the same exactly or come as near as their use will permit; as is seen particularly in the fabrick of Man's Body, his master-piece, whereof all the original parts have somewhat of the Spherical or Cylindrical Figure, which is the production of a Circle." [6] It was not by chance that the utopian metropolis of the mystical philosopher Campanella was laid out by city planners in circular form, "divided into seven rings or huge circles named from the seven planets," its thoroughfares four radii of the circle, leading toward the four points of the compass. At the center of the concentric rings stood a great domed temple, at whose center again were other circles, one globe representing the heavens, another the globe of our earth.

Among Renaissance artists the circle was as persistent as among the poets. No northern painter seems to have felt its religious and cosmic significance more deeply than the Flemish Pieter Bruegel the Elder. In his *View of the Harbour of Naples*, "the idea of the round, of the circle, dominates the landscape as much as the figure painting, and transmits the feeling of the huge vault of the globe to the spectator." One of his drawings in the Albertina shows Christ entering Limbo, "enclosed in a sphere of light with an angel's orchestra which rolls and floats through gorges between tremendous masks like a soap bubble." In the *Parable of the Wise and Foolish Virgins*, "the Virgins' earthly life rolls off in a realism comparable to Shakespeare's popular scenes. It rotates in bulky circles: at the right, the round-dance of the Foolish Virgins; at the left, the pious work of the Wise Virgins, bent over the mighty rounds of reel, tub, and basket. . . . The circular rhythm goes through everything." The circle is persistent

[6] *A General Collection of Discourses*, ed. by George Havers (London, 1673).

in Bruegel's extraordinary *Battle of the Angels and Demons:* in the "huge sun in a pale yellow glare, representing the celestial sphere," from which angels and demons stream out in concentric arches, "spreading like the waves of sound in the atmosphere." [7] It is definitely repeated in the smaller circles, arcs, and parabolas of the heads, wings, and shells of that strange profusion of fishes and lizards, dragonflies and bats, lobsters and crabs, perhaps spawned out by the demons, hybrid monsters that have interchanged their bodies, heads, and wings, more monstrously grotesque than Milton's vision of Hell:

> A universe of death, which God by curse
> Created evil, for evil only good;
> Where all life dies, death lives, and Nature breeds,
> Perverse, all monstrous, all prodigious things,
> Abominable, inutterable, and worse
> Than fables yet have feigned, or fear conceived,
> Gorgons, and Hydras, and Chimaeras dire. (*PL*, II.622–27)

Whether in the shape of the world or the shape of man's head, in mystical architecture like Campanella's or in such symbolism as Bruegel's, men saw the circle that had long been read into cyclical theories of human and political history. Man's life was a circle, from the womb to the grave: "Art thou loath to make up that circle with returning to the earth again?" asked Donne. Like men, nations had their periods of rise and of fall. "The lives, not only of men, but of Commonwealths, and the whole World," said Sir Thomas Browne, "run not upon an Helix that still enlargeth, but on a Circle, where, arriving to their Meridian, they decline in obscurity, and fall under the Horizon again." [8] Fortune,

[7] Otto Benesch, *Art of the Renaissance*, pp. 91–99.
[8] *Religio Medici*, I.17 (Keynes ed., I, 24).

whom the Romans had sometimes pictured as standing on a sphere, became in medieval times the goddess Fortuna with her familiar wheel on which men—and sometimes even Fortune herself—were whirled around. Both men and nations might have their ascendant periods, but time conquered all; and the Wheel of Fortune came full-circle.

Pondering upon God and man, seventeenth-century poets sought the circle as Browne the quincunx, and in their more serious moods read into it religious meaning. It was often, as with Milton, the symbol of the creation of the universe and of the world. George Sandys wrote:

> O Thou who All things hast of Nothing made,
> Whose Hand the radiant Firmament display'd;
> With such an undiscerned swiftness hurl'd
> About the stedfast Centre of the World;
> Against whose rapid course the restless Sun
> And wandring Flames in varied Motions run;
> Which Heat, Light, Life infuse.   (*Deo Opt. Max.*)

Drummond thought of the ascended Christ rising in glory through circles as intricate and as mystical as the wheels of Ezekiel's chariot:

> He towers those golden bounds
> He did to Sun bequeath,
> The higher wandering rounds
>   Are found his feet beneath;
>   The milky-way comes near,
>   Heavens axle seems to bend
>   Above each turning sphere
> That robed in glorie heaven's King may ascend.
>   (*An Hymne of the Ascension*)

Conscious of the perfection of God's universe and the imperfections of the world, Henry Vaughan

    gron'd to know
  Who gave the clouds so brave a bow,
  Who bent the spheres, and circled in
  Corruption with this glorious Ring.   (*Vanity of Spirit*)

But Thomas Traherne felt himself a little copy of the Great Circle:

    I was an Inward Sphere of Light,
  Or an Interminable Orb of Sight,
    An Endless and a Living Day,
  A vital Sun that round about did ray,
    All life and sence,
  A naked simple pure Intelligence. (*The Preparative*)

 Frequently poets used as a symbol of life the bubble—round, fragile, evanescent. "The world's a bubble, and the life of man / Less than a span," wrote Francis Bacon in one of his few attempts at verse. Drummond's *Madrigal* was defter:

  This life which seems so fair
  Is like a bubble blown up in the air
  By sporting children's breath,
  Who chase it everywhere,
  And strive who can most motion it bequeath.
  And though it seem sometime of its own might,
  Like to an eye of gold, to be fixed there,
  And firm to hover in that empty height,
  That only is because it is too slight.
  But in that pomp it doth not long appear,
    For even when most admired, it is a thought
    As swelled from nothing, doth dissolve in nought.

The most familiar seventeenth-century circle-poem is one of the loveliest—Henry Vaughan's *The World:*

I saw Eternity the other night,
Like a great Ring of pure and endless light,
    All calm as it was bright,
And round beneath it, Time in hours, days, years,
    Driv'n by the spheres,
Like a vast shadow mov'd in which the world
    And all her train were hurl'd.

I

But the circle did not always lead men's thoughts to God and eternity. One of the greatest charms of the seventeenth-century poets lay in their virtuosity in adapting their figures of speech to varying moods and music. They had the same fun with the circle as they had with that "epitome" which might express their profoundest convictions of man's relation to God and to the universe and world. Indeed circle and "copy" often became one in their minds, in part because they saw in both the repetitions of their three worlds, in part because they were charmed by the small,

All trying by a love of littlenesse
To make abridgments, and to draw to lesse,
Even that nothing, which at first we were.[9]

We shall better understand their first reactions to the vastness of the new universe if we realize that these were poets who loved flowers and birds and hills but felt little response to the wild and the grand in natural scenery. Like Sir Thomas Browne they went to school "to the wisdom of Bees, Ants and Spiders," and agreed with him that "Ruder heads stand

[9] John Donne, *To the Countesse of Salisbury*. I have quoted the lines out of their context.

amazed at those prodigious pieces of Nature, Whales, Ele-
phants, Dromidaries and Camels; these, I confess, are the
Colossus and majestick pieces of her hand; but in these narrow Engines there is more curious Mathematicks; and the
civility of these little Citizens more neatly sets forth the Wisdom of their Maker." [10] "I confess," wrote Abraham Cowley
lightly, "I love Littleness almost in all things. A little convenient Estate, a little cheerful House, a little Company, and
a very little Feast." He added: "If I were ever to fall in love
again (which is a great Passion, and therefore, I hope, I have
done with it) it would be, I think, with Prettiness, rather than
with Majestical Beauty." [11]

Changes upon the "epitome" or "small copy" could be
rung indefinitely by wits who felt the same ingenuous pleasure in the decreasing smallness of things as does a student
learning for the first time about *progression ad infinitum*.
Lovelace saw an epitome of mankind in *A Fly Caught in a
Cobweb,*

> Small type of great ones, that do hum
> Within this whole world's narrow room.

John Earle discovered copy after copy in his *Microcosmographia;* England was an epitome of the world, and
"Paul's walk is the land's epitome, or you may call it the lesser
isle of Great Britain." Perhaps the British played with the
conceit even more delightedly because they were themselves
islanders, living on a small copy of a continent, itself a copy of
the world. In the triple-talk at the beginning of Fletcher's
Purple Island, we are never quite sure whether it is the world,

[10] *Religio Medici,* I.xv (Keynes ed., I, 20).
[11] *Of Greatness,* in *Essays, Plays and Sundry Verses,* ed. by A. R. Waller
(Cambridge, 1906), p. 429.

the body of man, or "this blessed Isle, this England" that
God created,

> Then plac't it in the calm pacifick seas,
> And bid nor waves, nor troublous windes offend it;
> Then peopled it with subjects apt to please
> So wise a Prince, made able to defend it
> > Against all outward force, or inward spite;
> > Him framing like himself, all shining bright,
> A little living Sunne, Sonne of the living Light. (1.40)

England was the world's epitome in Waller's *Instructions to
a Painter*, whom he bade, "First draw the sea, that portion
which between / The greater world and this of ours is seen,"
and in his *Panegyric to my Lord Protector*:

> Our little world, the image of the great,
> Like that, amidst the boundless ocean set,
> Of her own growth hath all that Nature craves,
> And all that's rare, as tribute from the waves.

Crashaw too wrote of England in his lines *Upon the Kings
Coronation*:

> > doe I not see
> In this blest earth heavens bright Epitome,
> Circled with pure refined glory? heere
> I view a rising sunne in this our sphaere,
> Whose blazing beames, maugre the blackest night,
> And mists of greife, dare force a joyfull light.

Books were "little copies" with infinite riches in a narrow
room: "Indeed the world's thy book, Where all things have
their leafe assigned." Man himself was a book, the Book of
Nature or the Book of God. "The World is a great Volume,
and man the Index of that Booke; Even in the Body of Man,

you may turne to the whole world." [12] Emblem books were
epitomes of wisdom, for "An Emblem is but a silent parable.
. . . Before the knowledge of letters God was known by
hieroglyphics. And indeed what are the heavens, the earth,
nay every creature, but Hieroglyphics and Emblems of his
Glory?" [13] Printed books, too, were "epitomes" and "copies"
—it was a favorite inscription of authors. Crashaw wrote *On
a Prayer-Booke:*

> It is one rich handfull, heaven and all,
>   Heavens royall Hoasts incampt, thus small;
>   To prove that true, schooles used to tell
> A thousand Angells in one point can dwell;

and Lovelace of a very different kind of book, *Clitophen
and Lucippe Translated:*

> 'Tis an Abstract of all Volumnes,
> A Pillaster of all Columnes,
> Fancy e're rear'd to Wit, to be
> The smallest Gods Epitome,
> And so compactedly expresse
> All Lovers pleasing Wretchedness.

Most of all the child was an epitome, a little copy of the
little copy of the world and God. "A Child," said John Earle,
"is a man in small letter, yet the best copy of Adam before he
tasted of Eve or the Apple." In the *Winter's Tale* Paulina
saw the father in the child:

> Although the print be little, the whole matter
> And copy of the father—eye, nose, lip;
> The trick of's frown, his forehead . . .

[12] Donne, *Sermons,* ed. by L. P. Smith (Oxford, 1920), p. 67.
[13] Francis Quarles, *To the Reader,* in *Emblems,* ed. by George Gilfillan
(Edinburgh, 1857).

Crashaw in his panegyric *Upon the Duke of Yorke his Birth,* praised Charles in praising the infant copy:

See, see, thy reall shadow, see thy Brother,
Thy little selfe in lesse, read in these Eyne
The beames that dance in those full starres of thine.
From the same snowy Alabaster Rocke
These hands and thine were hew'n, these cherryes mocke
The Corall of thy lips. Thou art of all
This well-wrought Copy the faire Principall.

Watching *Princesse Löysa Drawing,* Lovelace thought he "saw a little Deity, Minerva in Epitomy." He found an epitome of the universe in the circle of *The Snayl:*

Wise emblem of our politick world,
Sage Snayl, within thine own self curl'd,
Instruct me softly to make hast,
Whilst these my feet go slowly fast.

Compendious Snayl! thou seem'st to me
Large Euclid's strict Epitome;
And in each diagram dost fling
Thee from the point unto the ring.
A figure now triangulare,
An oval now, and now a square,
And then a serpentine, dost crawl,
Now a straight line, now crook'd, now all. . . .

Who shall a name for thee create,
Deep riddle of mysterious state? . . . .
Thou, thine own daughter, then, and sire,
That son and mother art intire,
That big still with thy self dost go,
And li'vst an aged embrio.

Upon the circle, as upon the epitome, the poets rang their changes, from somber to gay. If they read into it sincere beliefs, they were equally capable of juggling their shining balls in the air, playing in *L'Allegro* mood, with quips and cranks and wanton wiles. "What's this *ducdame?*" Amiens asked as Jaques finished his catch. The seventeenth-century poets seem to reply with Jaques: " 'Tis a Greek invocation to call fools into a circle"—a circle of delightful foolery and metaphysical wit.

Donne was never more serious than when he set down memories of his nearly fatal illness in the meditations and prayers of his *Devotions,* but he could still smile as he remembered the giddiness of the first weak steps of convalescence:

I am up, and I seem to stand, and I go round; and I am a new argument of the new philosophy, that the earth moves round; why may I not believe that the whole earth moves in a round motion, though that seem to me to stand, when as I seem to stand to my company, and yet am carried, in a giddy and circular motion as I stand? [14]

Sir Thomas Browne discovered the circle in the "strange Cryptography" of the "Starry Book of Heaven." But he could find it equally in small and neglected things, in "those elegant Semicircles . . . in the Sea Hedge-hogge." The circles of the planets were not more admirable than those which this most "Studious Observator" of Nature discovered in one of the homeliest of his correspondences, "the circinations and sphaerical rounds of Onyons, wherein the circles of the orbes are ofttimes larger, and the meridionall lines stand wider upon one side then the other." [15]

[14] Meditation XXI, *Devotions upon Emergent Occasions* (London, 1840).
[15] *Garden of Cyrus*, III, IV (Keynes ed., IV, 101, 108).

Dante's God was the center of the Great Rose, but Thomas Heywood's was the chief spectator in the circular Globe Theatre:

> If then the World a Theater present,
> As by the roundnesse it appears most fit,
> Built with starre-galleries of hye ascent,
> In which Jehove doth as spectator sit.
>
> *(The Author to His Booke)*

As Sir John Davies found the perfection of the circle in the celestial, Milton in the angelic dance, Richard Lovelace saw the same symbolism in his mistress as he watched *Gratiana Dancing and Singing:*

> See! with what constant motion,
> Even and glorious as the sun,
>   Gratiana steers that noble frame,
> Soft as her breast, sweet as her voice,
> That gave each winding law and poise, . . .
>
> So did she move; so did she sing
> Like the harmonious spheres that bring
>   Unto their rounds their music's aid;
> Which she performed in such a way
> As all th' enamored world will say,
>   The Graces danced, and Apollo played.

William Strode discovered traces of the circle even in sheep-tracks on Westwell Downs:

> The sheep sometimes do tread a maze
> By often winding in and in,
> And sometimes round about them trace
> What milkmaids call a fairy ring;
>   Such semicircles they have run,

Such lines across so lively spun,
That shepherd's term whene'er they please
A new geometry with ease.   (*On Westwell Downs*)

Not entirely a "new geometry," perhaps, but never did poets play with mathematics more delightedly than in this age when Marvell could write in *The Definition of Love:*

As Lines so Loves oblique may well
Themselves in every Angle greet:
But ours so truly Paralel
Though infinite can never meet.

Deftly they adapted Euclid to dance, to flattery, to compliment, as well as to cosmology. In the masque of *Oberon* Ben Jonson paid tribute to the king, who "in his own true circle still doth run; / And holds his course as certain as the sun," and bade the "bright Faies and Elves"

turn your lays
Unto his name; then let your nimble feet
Treat subtle circles that may always meet
In point to him, and figures, to express
The grace of him and his great emperess.

Still more involved in an old rather than a new geometry was Jonson's adaptation of the seven liberal arts in his tribute to Michael Drayton, *A Vision of the Muses*. The beauty of Drayton's verse, like the newly risen sun,

fill'd an orb as circular as heaven;
This orb was cut forth into regions seven,
And these so sweet and well proportion'd parts
As it had been a circle of the arts.

Milton's Great Geometer used the golden compasses in the creation of the world. Ben Jonson's own "Impresa," we are told by Drummond of Hawthornden, was a "Compass with one foot in Center, the other Broken." Many a gentle-man of the period had his portrait painted in his study beside his globe, maps on the wall, compasses in hand. Poets used the compass-figure in various ways,[16] though most often they adapted either the mariner's or the geometer's compass to earthly love. Thomas Carew wrote "To Celia upon Love's Ubiquity":

> My whole life is 'bout you, the centre star,
> But a perpetual motion circular.
> I am the dial's hand, still walking round;
> You are the compass; and I never sound
> Beyond your circle, neither can I show
> Aught, but what first expressed is in you.

Donne, as we shall see, could read religious significance into the compass, yet in his most familiar compass-figure, in *A Valediction: Forbidding Mourning*, he was speaking not of God and man, but of man and woman:

> If they be two, they are two so
> As stiffe twin compasses are two,
> Thy soule, the fixt foot, makes no show
> To move, but doth, if th' other doe.

[16] Cf. George Wither, *A Collection of Emblems* (1633):

> For, as to draw a Circle, with our hand
> We cause the brazen Compasses to stand
> With one foot firmely fix'd on the ground;
> And move the other in a Constant round:
> Right so, when we shall purpose to proceed
> In any just, and profitable deed,
> We first should by a constant resolution
> Stand firme, to what we put in execution.

Otto Benesch, in *The Art of the Renaissance in Northern Europe*, fre-quently discusses the effect of mathematics upon the plastic art of the Renais-sance.

And though it in the center sit,
Yet when the other far doth rome,
It leanes and hearkens after it,
And growes erect, as that comes home.

Such wilt thou be to mee, who must
Like th' other foot, obliquely run;
Thy firmness draws my circle just,
And makes me end where I begun.

"Love à la Euclid" was satirized more than once, but no seventeenth-century poet had more fun with it than did John Cleveland in his parody on the scientifically amorous poets:

Mystical grammar of amorous glances;
Feeling of pulses, the physic of love;
Rhetorical courtings and musical dances;
Numb'ring of kisses arithmetic prove;
   Eyes like astronomy;
   Straight-limbed geometry;
   In her art's ingeny
   Our wits were sharp and keen.
      Never Mark Antony
      Dallied more wantonly
      With the fair Egyptian Queen.[17]

Nevertheless, in spite of the "geometricians," the circle-figure was well adapted to the language of love, for as Herrick said,

Love is a circle that doth restless move
In the same sweet eternity of love,

while Quarles changed the familiar figure to, "Love the circumference was, and love the center." The circle was a favorite figure of courtly compliment to Lord Herbert of Cherbury, who wrote to the Countess of Denbigh,

[17] *Mark Antony,* in *Minor Poets of the Caroline Period,* III, 70.

> in your face, as in a beauteous sphere,
> Delight and state so sweetly mix'd appear,

and flattered *A Lady who did Sing Excellently* by finding the harmony of beauty in both her features and her song:

> When again all these rare perfections meet,
> Composed in the circle of thy face,
>   As in their place,
> So as to make up of all one perfect sweet,
> Who is not then so ravish'd with delight,
>   Ev'n of thy sight?

Waller wrote charming lines upon his mistress' girdle, deftly inscribing one circle in another:

> That which her slender waist confined
> Shall now my joyful temples bind:
> No monarch but would give his crown,
> His arms might do what this has done.
>
> It was my Heaven's extremst sphere,
> The pale which held that lovely deer;
> My joy, my grief, my hope, my love
> Did all within this circle move.
>
> A narrow compass! and yet there
> Dwelt all that's good, and all that's fair;
> Give me but what this ribband bound,
> Take all the rest the sun goes round.

II

Of all the minor circle-figures of the century, none was more persistent than the tears that flowed so easily and copiously from the eyes of seventeenth-century lovers and their ladies. "Holy Gonzalo," said Prospero, "Mine eyes, even sociable to the show of thine, / Fall fellowly tears." One longs to collect those tears of the past in a vial worthy their sparkling sadness, as did Marvell:

> I in a golden Vial will
> Keep these two crystal Tears; and fill
> It till it do o'reflow
> (*The Nymph complaining for the Death of her Faun*)

or in Donne's vial to test all lovers' tears against one's own,

> Hither with cristall vyals, lovers come,
> And take my teares, which are loves wine,
> And try your Mistresse Tears at home,
> For all are false that tast not just like mine.
> (*Twicknam Garden*)

In *Mourning* Marvell watched a lady weeping for her dead lover:

> Her Eyes confus'd and doubled ore,
> With Tears suspended ere they flow,
> Seem bending upwards, to restore
> To Heaven, whence it came, their Woe.
>
> When molding of the watry Sphears,
> Slow drops unty themselves away;
> As if she, with those precious Tears,
> Would strow the ground where Strephon lay.

Even more moving to Marvell was the nymph, complaining for the death of her fawn, whose round tears mingled with those of her dying pet:

> See how it weeps. The Tears do come,
> Sad, slowly dropping like a Gumme.

So weeps the wounded Balsame; so
The holy Frankincense doth flow.

In *Eyes and Tears* Marvell's metaphysical love-tears seem
curiously like medicinal pellets weighed on an apothecary's
scale:

Two Tears, which Sorrow long did weigh
Within the Scales of either Eye,
And then paid out in equal Poise
Are the true price of all my Joyes.

Carew in *A Looking Glass* watched his own tears, shed for a
lady who did not deserve them:

About your cold heart they did make
A circle, where the briny lake
Congeal'd into a crystal cake.

In less personal mood, he wrote an epitaph for *A Fly that
Flew into my Mistress' Eye:*

At last into her eye she flew,
There, scorch'd in heat and drown'd in dew,
Like Phaethon from the sun's sphere
She fell, and with her dropp'd a tear:
Of which a pearl was straight composed,
Wherein her ashes lie enclosed.

William Strode—the poet of the sheep-tracks—varied the figure as he watched *Chloris Walking in the Snow:*

The wanton snow flew to her breast
Like little birds into their nest,
But overcome with whiteness there,
For grief it thawed into a tear,
Then folding down her garment hem
        To deck her, froze into a gem.

Donne too loved the "sweet salt tears" of lovers which flowed in such profusion that on more than one occasion they threatened to engulf the globe:

> Oft a flood
> Have we two wept, and so
> Drowned the whole World, us two.

"Let me powre forth / My teares before thy face," he begged in *A Valediction: Of Weeping*. Each of his mistress' tears was a copy of the globe, the combined tears of lover and lady a symbol of the Deluge that had once destroyed it:

> On a round ball
> A workeman that hath copies by, can lay
> An Europe, Afrique, and an Asiä,
> And quickly make that, which was nothing, *ALL*,
> So doth each teare,
> Which thee doth weare,
> A globe, yea world by that impression grow,
> Till thy teares mixt with mine doe overflow
> This world, by waters sent from thee, my heaven disolved so.

"Powre new seas in my eyes," he wrote in different vein in a *Holy Sonnet*, "that so I might / Drowne my world with my weeping earnestly."

"Tears, flow no more, or if you needs must flow, / Fall yet more slow," urged Herbert of Cherbury; "Do not the world invade." But Richard Crashaw heeded no such warning. No poet of the century collected more tears in his angelic "crystal phials" than did the *Weeper* of the

> two faithful fountains,
> Two walking baths, two weeping motions,
> Portable and compendious oceans,

who should have said of himself rather than of Mary Magdalene,

> O precious prodigal!
>   Fair spend-thrift of thyself! . . .
> All places, times, and objects be
> Thy tears' sweet opportunity.

Like contemporary love-poets, Crashaw sometimes used lay-figures, seeing round tears in a shooting-star about to fall, in a pearl slipt from Aurora's breast, in the "Sweet lip kisses" of the rosebud. But religious tears were more characteristic of him:

> What bright soft thing is this?
> Sweet Mary, thy faire Eyes expence?
>   A moist sparke it is,
> A watry Diamond; from whence
> The very Terme, I think, was found,
> The water of a Diamond.   (*The Teare*)

In the symbolism of *The Waters of our Lords Baptisme*, he saw the circle:

> Each blest drop, on each blest limme,
> Is wash'd it selfe, in washing him;
> 'Tis a Gemme, while it stayes here,
> When it falls hence, 'tis a Teare.

Sometimes restrained within the limits of the Circle of Perfection, Crashaw's "ever-watry eyes" more often overflowed all bounds, making the poet—as he said of the dead Bishop Andrewes—"all one great Eye, all drown'd in one great Teare." In his religious poetry, his favorite lachrymal symbols were the "fair floods," the "sister springs," and all

> Ever-bubling things!
> Thawing crystall! snowy hills,
> Still spending, never spent!   (*The Weeper*)

But Crashaw's circles were not always lugubrious. His poetry indeed was a "sweet Contest of woes with loves; of teares with smiles disputing." If he never went as far as did Carew, who in an *Elegy* instructed the Muse to "Dry up her blubbered eyes, and learn to smile," smile Crashaw could. Remembering the primitive earth, when all was fresh and fair, he saw the circle as a symbol of spring:

> Nor doe I doubt
> But when the world first out of Chaos sprang
> So smil'd the Dayes, and so the tenor ran
>   Of their felicity. A spring was there,
> An everlasting spring; the jolly yeare
> Led round in his great circle, . . .
>   (*Out of Virgil: In the praise of the Spring*)

As in the past, so in the world to come, the circle would again be a symbol of happiness:

> when weake Time shall be pour'd out
> Into Eternity, and circular joyes
> Dance in an endlesse round, againe shall rise
> The faire son of an ever-youthfull spring.
>   (*Upon the Death of Mr. Herrys*)

In his hymn *In the Glorious Epiphanie of our Lord God*, the "Bright Babe, Whose awfull beautyes make / The morn incurr a sweet mistake" was symbolic of the vastness of the macrocosm's "all-circling point, / All centring Sphear," but to Crashaw the Babe was a tender symbol, too, of our world lying safe within the everlasting arms:

O little all! in thy embrace
The world lyes warm and likes his place.
Nor does his full Globe fail to be
Kist on both his cheeks by Thee.
Time is too narrow for thy Year,
Nor makes the whole World thy half-sphear.

III

No poet of the seventeenth century used the circle more charmingly than did Andrew Marvell. He loved it for its beauty of form, whether he found it in the tears of a lady or a pet fawn, in a cherry or an "onion root" like Browne's, or discovered it in a more exotic Nature in his *Garden,* with the "Nectaren and curious Peach," the "ripe Apples," and the symbolic "melon," a combination of Sappho's apple and Eve's, stumbling on which man fell on grass. In the "remote Bermoothes," he liked to think that tropical Nature was expressed in circles. There God

> hangs in shades the Orange bright,
> Like golden Lamps in a green Night,
> And does in the Pomegranate close
> Jewels more rich than Ormus show's.
> He makes the Figs our mouths to meet,
> And throws the Melons at our feet.   (*Bermudas*)

The Circle of Perfection, read into Nature by God, is a clue to Marvell's ethics and aesthetics, to both of which limitation, restraint, proportion were basic. Praising Appleton House, he condemned all that was unrestrained and disproportionate in architecture:

> Why should of all things Man unrul'd
> Such unproportion'd dwellings build?

> The Beasts are by their Denns exprest:
> The Birds contrive an equal Nest;
> The low roof'd Tortoises do dwell
> In cases fit of Tortoise-shell.   (*Upon Appleton House*, 11)

In Appleton House he found the ethical order and restraint
he considered essential to beauty:

> But all things are composed here
> Like Nature, orderly and near;
> In which we the Dimensions find
> Of that more sober Age and Mind,
> When larged sized Men did stoop
> To enter at a narrow loop;
> As practising, in doors so strait,
> To strain themselves through Heavens Gate.   (iv)

His poem *Upon the Hill and Grove of Billbarrow* echoes his
distaste for the irregular, the formless, the unconstrained in
Nature, symbolized in the "proud mountains"

> That do with your hook-shoulder'd height
> The earth deform and heaven fright,
> For whose excrescence, ill designed,
> Nature must a new Center find.

His own ideal of beauty he found rather in the perfect symmetry of the hill at Billbarrow:

> See how the archéd Earth does here
> Rise in a perfect Hemisphere!
> The stiffest compass could not strike
> A line more circular and like;
> Nor softest Pensel draw a brow
> So equal as this Hill does bow.
> It seems as for a Model laid,
> And that the World by it was made.

Ethically and aesthetically his lesson is always one of restraint, proportion, moderation, humility, a lesson he characteristically expressed in the mathematical terms of his century. Others attempted to square the circle; God's circle of beauty and truth was enough for Andrew Marvell:

> Humility alone designs
> Those short but admirable Lines,
> By which, ungirt and unconstrain'd,
> Things greater are in less contain'd.
> Let others vainly strive t'immure
> The Circle in the Quadrature!
> These holy Mathematicks can
> In ev'ry Figure equal Man.   (*Upon Appleton House*, vi)

In the loveliest circle-poem of the seventeenth century, Marvell brought to poetic climax the long belief in epitomes and correspondences, the mirroring of the macrocosm in a microcosm. The Circle of Perfection was breaking when Marvell wrote, yet it had lost none of its cosmic significance to him. His subject in *On a Drop of Dew* was only the morning dew in the heart of a flower, but as Tennyson sought the meaning of God and man in a flower in a crannied wall, and Blake found "a world in a grain of sand and a heaven in a wild flower," Marvell saw the universe reflected in a drop of dew:

> See how the Orient Dew,
> Shed from the Bosom of the Morn
>   Into the blowing Roses,
> Yet careless of its Mansion new;
> For the clear Region where 'twas born
>   Round in it self incloses:
>   And in its little Globes Extent,

Frames as it can its native Element.
How it the purple flow'r does slight,
Scarce touching where it lyes,
But gazing back upon the Skies,
Shines with a mournful Light;
Like its own Tear,
Because so long divided from the Sphear.

Restless it roules and unsecure,
Trembling lest it grow impure:
Till the warm Sun pitty it's Pain,
And to the Skies exhale it back again
So the Soul, that Drop, that Ray
Of the clear Fountain of Eternal Day,
Could it within the humane flow'r be seen,
Remembering still its former height,
Shuns the sweet leaves and blossoms green;
And, recollecting its own Light,
Does, in its pure and circling thoughts, express
The greater Heaven in an Heaven less.

Marvell's circle-images are more beautiful than Donne's, yet not even Marvell was as obsessed with the circle as was Donne, who deserves the final place in this essay both because of the profusion and intricacy of his circle-images, and because he was the first of the seventeenth-century poets to realize that, even as he wrote, the circle was breaking. In his early love-poetry, as we have seen, Donne played lightly with the symbol. In *The Token* he begged of his lady no conventional token, "noe ribbond wrought with thine owne handes,"

nor Ring to shew the stands
Of our affection, that as that's round and plaine
So should our loves meet in simplicity.

When another mistress returned to him a ring, he remembered that the jet ring was "nor halfe so brittle as her heart," and mused:

> Yet stay with mee since thou art come,
> Circle this fingers top, which did'st her thombe.
> Be justly proud, and gladly safe, that thou dost dwell with me,
> She that, Oh, broke her faith, would soon breake thee.
>
> (*A Jeat Ring Sent*)

Pondering somewhat more seriously upon love, he thought of circles in water:

> If, as in water stir'd more circles bee
> Produc'd by one, love such additions take,
> Those like so many spheares, but one heaven make,
> For, they are all concentrique unto thee.   (*Loves Growth*)

But although the younger Donne frequently used the circle-figure—as we have seen in the *Valediction: Of Weeping*, in which the lovers' tears became symbols of the globe and the Deluge, and in the *Valediction: Forbidding Mourning*, with its elaborate compass-figure—the earlier poet of love and laughter showed no such feeling for the symbolism of the circle as did the later John Donne who read into it more involved meanings than any other poet of the century. The compass-figure appears in a different connotation in *Obsequies to the Lord Harrington*:

> O Soule, O circle, why so quickly bee
> Thy ends, thy birth and death, clos'd up in thee?
> Since one foot of thy compasse still was plac'd
> In heav'n; the other might securely have pac'd
> In the most large extent, through every path,
> Which the whole world, or man the abridgement hath.

From the compass, Donne's "curious mind" went on to other circles large and small: "small pocket-clocks, whose every wheele / Doth each mismotion and distemper feel"; "great clocks, which in steeples chime"; "sun-dyalls"; the greater and smaller circles marked upon those globes on which a workman might "lay an Europe, Afrique, and an Asia":

> Thou knowst, that though the tropique circles have
> (Yea and those small ones which the Poles engrave,)
> All the same roundnesse, evennesse, and all
> The endlessnesse of the equinoctiall;
> Yet, when we come to measure distances,
> How here, how there, the Sunne affected is,
> When he doth faintly worke, and when prevaile,
> Onely great circles then can be our scale.

Later, in the *Devotions*, he returned to the compass-figure to illustrate man's need of God as the true "centre":

As he that would describe a circle in paper, if he have brought that circle within one inch of finishing, yet if he remove his compass, he cannot make it into a perfect circle, except he fall to work again, to find out the same centre, so, though setting that foot of my compass upon thee, I have gone so far as to the consideration of myself, yet if I depart from thee, my centre all is imperfect.

(*Expostulation* xx)

Other geometrical figures sprang often to his mind, as to the minds of other Euclidean poets:

> Know that all lines which circles doe containe,
> For once that they the Center touch, doe touch
> Twice the circumference. (*Second Anniversary*, ll. 436–38)

In one of his verse-letters of instruction, he bade the Countess of Bedford remember that, in the truly religious, religion radiates outward from the center:

> In those poor types of God (round circles) so
> Religious tipes, the peecelesse centers flow,
> And are in all the lines which all wayes goe.

Like Marvell, he inveighed against those who rhetorically sought to square the Circle, which is God:

> Eternall God, (for whom who ever dare
> Seeke new expressions, doe the Circle square,
> And thrust into strait corners of poore wit
> Thee, who art cornerlesse and infinite.)
>   (*Upon the Translation of the Psalms by Sir Philip Sidney*)

"Perfect motions are all circular," he wrote to the Countess of Bedford. On the occasion of one of his journeys, as we have seen, he saw the cross reflected everywhere, but when on Good Friday, 1613, he was "riding westward," his metaphysical mind played with the circle:

> Let mans Soule be a Sphaere, and then, in this,
> The intelligence that moves, devotion is,
> And as the other Sphaeres, by being growne
> Subject to forraigne motions, lose their owne,
> And being by others hurried every day,
> Scarce in a yeare their naturall forme obey:
> Pleasure or business, so, our Soules admit
> For their first mover, and are whirld by it.
> Hence is't, that I am carryed towards the West
> This day, when my Soules forme bends toward the East.
> There I should see a Sunne, by rising set,
> And by that setting endless day beget. . . .
> Could I behold those hands which span the Poles,
> And turne all sphaeres at once, peirc'd with those holes?
>   (*Riding Westward*)

The circle was man's symbol, since death was the meeting of two ends of a circle, the first in the womb, the second in the grave. But most of all, to the religious Donne, the circle was the symbol of God. "O Eternall and most gracious God," he wrote in a prayer in his *Devotions*, "who, considered in thy selfe, art a Circle, first and last, and altogether." In the circles of his own world and in the convexity of the heavens, Donne discovered the "Hieroglyphick" of a God whose sun and moon and stars moved circularly, who had made all things in earth and in man as nearly perfect as their terrestrial limitations would permit, who had expressed His Nature both in the heavens and in the final resolution of the finite circle of the round earth into infinity at the Last Judgment:

> At the round earths imagin'd corners, blow
> Your trumpets, Angells, and arise, arise
> From death, you numberlesse infinites
> Of soules, and to your scattred bodies goe.
>
> (*Holy Sonnets*, vII)

The "Hydroptique" and immoderate love of learning, so characteristic of his Renaissance inheritance, prepared John Donne for his unique position as the first English poet who experienced the full impact of that "new Philosophy" which for a time called "all in doubt." It prepared him too to anticipate, even though he did not fully comprehend, the final breaking of the Circle of Perfection which he had used with more complexity than did any other poet of his period. The advancement of learning in Donne's own lifetime proved the truth of words he once wrote lightly when a lady returned to him a jet ring: "Nothing so endlesse, nothing sooner broke."

3

THE DEATH OF A WORLD

There is no more somber poem in the English language than
Donne's threnody, *An Anatomie of the World*, a dirge upon
the decay and death of man, of the world, of the universe.
It was almost neglected even by enthusiasts who brought
Donne's earlier *Songs and Sonets* into fashion, perhaps because, stiff with paradox, cryptic with double and triple meanings, it is as difficult as it is morose. But the poem is much
more than a mere enigma. Embedded within it lies an "epitome" of the intellectual universe in which Donne lived during the years that saw his transformation from "Jack" Donne
to Dr. Donne, Dean of St. Paul's, and the transformation of
our world from medieval to modern. "Untwisting all the
chains that tie the hidden soul of harmony," a modern reader
will understand better than from any other one poem what
the Elizabethans had made of the world and the universe.
Macrocosm, geocosm, and microcosm, elements and humors,
correspondences—all the parts are there. Yet the whole is
more than mere sum of its parts. With the sequel, *Of the
Progres of the Soul*, the *Anniversaries* constitute one of the
great religious poems of the seventeenth century.

"Look here upon this picture, and on this," said Hamlet.
As they liked "companion-pictures" so men of the Renais-

sance liked "companion-poems." The *Anniversaries* are such poems, as artfully though not so obviously articulated as *L'Allegro* and *Il Penseroso*. The first is a lament over the body—the body of man and the body of the world—a meditation upon death and mortality. The second is a vision of the release of the soul from its prison. The whole, with antitheses of doubt and faith, despair and hope, death and the triumph of immortality, is a great symphony in which the harmony is more profound because of cacophony.

One theme of the poems—the symbolic relationship between the death of a woman and the death of the world—Donne had anticipated in *A Feaver*, when in youth he had faced the possible death of a mistress:

> But when thou from this world wilt goe,
>   The whole world vapors with thy breath.
> Or if, when thou, the worlds soule, goest,
>   It stay, tis but thy carkasse then.

These lines, which might be paralleled in those of many poets, had been written by "Jack" Donne. At a crucial period of his later personal and religious life, John Donne returned to the idea and set the theme for his longest poems in *A Funerall Elegie:*

> and shee
> Being spent, the world must needs decrepit bee;
> For since death will proceed to triumph still,
> He can finde nothing, after her, to kill,
> Except the world it selfe, so great as shee.   (Lines 29–33)

The circumstances of the poem are well known. When he wrote the *Funerall Elegie*, Donne was in severe financial straits as a result of his clandestine marriage, which had alienated the most important patrons of a day in which poets lived—if they lived at all as poets—upon patronage. Donne was also in a period of religious transition; born and reared a Roman Catholic, he had left his Mother Church; he had not yet taken orders in the Anglican Church. He was suffering his personal problems, his doubts and despairs, in a period of melancholy. Still seeking the patron he needed badly, he had reason to suspect that he might find him in Sir Robert Drury.[1]

In 1610 Sir Robert Drury's daughter died at the age of fifteen. Shortly after Elizabeth Drury's death, Donne wrote the *Elegie,* followed the next year by *An Anatomie of the World,* usually referred to today as *The First Anniversary.* The two poems he published together—his first real publications, since the *Songs and Sonets;* the *Satyres* and other earlier works had been circulated only in manuscript. Some time later,[2] when—the patronage he sought achieved—he was traveling on the continent with Sir Robert Drury, he composed what we now call *The Second Anniversary* and published the three parts as a whole. According to his own statement, he had intended to continue the elegies in succeeding years. Possibly he changed his plan because of the reception of the first two poems, particularly by the Elizabethan Great Cham. Drummond of Hawthornden, recalling his conversations with Ben

[1] Much more complete knowledge of the relationship between Donne and Sir Robert Drury is now available than was the case when I published the first edition of this study. R. C. Bald in *Donne and the Drurys* (Cambridge, 1959), has made a careful study of the Drury manuscripts, now in the collections of the University of Chicago, on the basis of which he presents new information and corrects various misinterpretations suggested in the past.

[2] Professor Bald has shown that various tales told about Elizabeth Drury's death, to one of which I referred in my earlier essay, were apocryphal. He also offers evidence to prove that the *Second Anniversary* was not written at the time of the second anniversary of the death, but much earlier, possibly even at the time of the first anniversary. As he says (p. 93), "Donne was paying his rent in advance."

Jonson, set down the dictator's opinion that the *Anniversary Poems* were "prophane and full of blasphemies; that he told Mr. Done if it had been written of the Virgine Marie it had been something; to which he answered that he described the Idea of a Woman, and not as she was." It seems to me more probable that Donne as an artist realized that his companion-poems were structurally and emotionally complete as they stood.[3]

Jonson's judgment has been shared by various modern critics. H. J. C. Grierson condemned their "execrable extravagancies," though he felt Donne's "passionate awareness of the transcendent" and his "fervor of inspiration," and recognized "amid much that is both puerile and extravagant, a loftier strain of impassioned reflection and vision."[4] Later critics remembered Grierson's strictures but forgot his sensitive praise. In the 1920s and 1930s the poems were defended, if at all, for their ideas by critics who often considered them poetically "a series of preposterous elegies." Some writers, indeed, in their attempts to explain the poems read into them blasphemies which might well have shocked John Donne himself as much as his supposed blasphemies shocked Ben Jonson. William Empson, for example, called the whole "an enormous picture of the complete decay of the universe . . . caused by the death of a girl of no importance whom Donne had never seen," and went on to say: "Only Christ would be enough; only his removal from the world would explain the

---

[3] In my earlier version I referred to an article by Louis I. Martz, "John Donne in Meditation: *The Anniversaries*," *E.L.H.*, XIV (1947), 247 ff., as the best study I had found of the structure of the poems. Since that time Professor Martz has further developed his ideas in his admirable volume *The Poetry of Meditation* (New Haven, 1954). His study of the structure of the *Anniversary* poems may be found in Part 2, chapter 6.

[4] Grierson, *The Poems of John Donne* (Oxford, 1912), pp. xxvii, xxx.

destruction foretold by astronomers. The only way to make the poem sensible is to accept Elizabeth Drury as the Logos." [5] Other critics, too, suggested that Donne deliberately read into a dead girl attributes of Christ.

Donne himself briefly discussed the criticism of his poems in a letter to George Gerrard, written in April, 1612: "Of my Anniversaries, the fault that I acknowledge in my self, is to have descended to print any thing in verse, which though it have excuse even in our own times by men who professe, and practise much gravitie; yet I confesse I wonder how I declined to it, and do not pardon my self." His mistake, in his own mind, had not been in writing but in publishing the poems. He continued: "But for the other part of the imputation of having said too much, my defence is, that my purpose was to say as well as I could; for since I never saw the Gentlewoman, I cannot be understood to have bound my self to have spoken just truths, but I would not be thought to have gone about to praise her, or any other in rime; except I took such a person, as might be capable of all that I could say." Elizabeth Drury was a legitimate enough point of departure for a Renaissance poet who wished to use the death of an individual symbolically. She was "capable" of what Donne intended to say, in that she had died in "white innocence"; "cloath'd in

[5] Empson, *English Pastoral Poetry* (New York, 1938), p. 84. Mr. Martz, in the article referred to above, says on p. 258: "Donne here attempts to treat the girl in the convention of profane poetry of compliment, at the same time giving her the powers of a Christ." Cf. Charles Monroe Coffin, *John Donne and the New Philosophy* (New York, 1938), p. 276: "This is the heavy burden of religion and philosophy shouldered upon the fragile story of the life and death of Elizabeth Drury. Unless we recognize in her brief encounter with human experience the lofty parallel to the incarnation of Christ himself, Donne's attempt is hopeless—and for many this will but emphasize the doubtfulness of his taste." Mr. Coffin says again, on p. 258: "Though Christ is not named in either of the *Anniversaries*, He is definitely figured forth as Elizabeth Drury."

her virgin white integritie," she might fittingly serve as a symbol of "Vertue attir'd in woman."

But Elizabeth Drury was only a point of departure, an occasion for Donne's pondering upon far more universal problems than those involved in the death of any individual. To read the poem on one level, as did Jonson, is to miss both the poet's meaning and his art. Donne might well have replied to Ben Jonson that his poem *was* about the Virgin Mary, and might have added that the dead "Elizabeth" he celebrated was less a fifteen-year-old girl he had never seen than the Virgin Queen, whose recent death had marked the end of an era. "Shee, shee is dead; shee's dead": this is the refrain of both *Anniversary* poems, reiterated at the end of each section, emphasizing the form and structure of the whole. "Shee is dead" —and with her is dying the world; "shee" has left the earth, and with her have gone cherished values, beauty, purity, justice, truth:

> 'Tis all in peeces, all cohaerence gone;
> All just supply, and all Relation.   (*FA*, ll. 213–14)

"Some moneths she hath been dead," Donne wrote; but his mind went on at once to a deeper level of meaning:

> But long she 'ath beene away, long, long, yet none
> Offers to tell us who it is that's gone.   (*FA*, ll. 41–42)

Right there the trouble lies, I think, so far as interpreters of the poem are concerned: "none offers to tell us *who* it is that's gone." Elizabeth Drury had been dead for only a few months: but who is "shee," persistently the refrain of the poem, who "hath beene away, long, long?"

Cryptic though he was, Donne was always a fair player at the Renaissance game of riddles and double-meanings, scrupulously giving clues to his enigmas. Yet no modern critic appears to notice one that seems to me most important. It has been taken for granted that the apparent vacillation between "she" and "shee" throughout the poems was merely the result of Donne's Elizabethan vagaries or those of his printers. I am persuaded that the differentiation between "she" and "shee" was as deliberate as it is consistent.[6] Scholars have shown that, unlike many of his contemporaries who were careless about such matters, Donne was a stickler for punctuation, and—in the few works which he himself prepared for the press—tried to make the printers follow his marks, rather than their own Elizabethan and Jacobean caprices. In the *Anniversary Poems*, I believe that Donne was equally careful to see that the printer followed him in the spelling of that important pronoun, which is a main key to the structure and interpretation of the poem. In one of his verse-letters to the Countess of Bedford, written when she had lost her "other half" in the death of her closest friend, Donne wrote: "You that are *she*, and you, that's *double shee*." The italics are mine, but the distinction was his. The difference between "she" and what I call "double shee" holds good throughout both *Anniversaries*, and may briefly be stated thus: when Donne uses the more common "she," he is speaking of a real person.

[6] As I indicated in my earlier comments, I am fully aware of the danger of such an hypothesis as I offer, when it is based upon printed texts of the seventeenth century. Nevertheless we have evidence that in other works published during his lifetime, Donne was not only careful but even stubbornly insistent that the printer follow his manuscripts with care. Professor Grierson, although he grants that Donne's manuscripts were more carefully edited than those of various other writers of the time, nevertheless challenged my interpretation both in correspondence and in his review of *The Breaking of the Circle* in *Modern Language Review*, XLVII (1952), 390–92. Joan Bennett in her review (*Review of English Studies*, N.S. III [1952], 178–80) suggests that the difference in spelling indicates the stress Donne wished the syllable to have in pronunciation.

When he uses the "double shee," he is writing in symbolic, universal, and abstract terms about what he himself called "the Idea of a Woman."

The difference in spelling of the specific and the general is not peculiar to the *Anniversary Poems*, though it is most consistent and important in them. The problem in reading any such interpretation out of the earlier poems arises, as I realize, from the fact that they were not published in Donne's lifetime and that, while various manuscripts are extant, none is in his own hand. Perhaps he himself had always made a distinction between single and double endings, though I think that the usage developed slowly in his mind, as he dwelt with more serious themes. In the early poems, as they have been printed, there is often no difference in meaning implied in the use of the final double-letter, except in so far as "shee, hee, wee, bee" are frequently used for rhyme with "thee." On the other hand, Nature, as an abstraction, is usually "shee," and God, with only two or three exceptions, is "Hee." Donne seems to have made a deliberate distinction between the spelling of person and idea in *The Legacie* when he wrote:

> I heard *mee* say, Tell her anon,
>> That my selfe (that is you, not I,)
>> Did kill *me*, and when I felt *mee* dye,
> I bid *mee* send my heart, when I was gone,
> But I alas could there finde none,
>> When I had ripp'd me, and search'd where hearts did
>> lye;
>> It kill'd *mee* againe, *that I who still was true*.[7]

The implications of the single and double endings in *The Extasie* closely parallel those in the *Anniversaries*:

[7] In this passage and those that immediately follow the italics are mine.

> Where, like a pillow on a bed,
>   A Pregnant banke swel'd up, to rest
> The violets reclining head,
>   Sat *we* two, one anothers best.

The lovers are still in the body; they are persons. But when "our soules . . . were gone out," and the lovers sublimated in ecstasy to a transcendent One,

> *Wee* like sepulchral statues lay;
> All day, the same our postures were,
>   And *wee* said nothing, all the day.

The distinction between body and spirit, individual and idea, is clear in the climactic lines:

> *Wee* then, who are this new soule, know,
>   Of what we are compos'd, and made,
> For th' Atomies of which *we* grow
>   Are soules, whom no change can invade.
> But O alas, so long, so farre
>   Our bodies why doe *wee* forbeare?
> They are ours, though they are not *wee*, *Wee* are
>   The intelligences, they the sphaere.

I shall not labor the early poems, however, since we have insufficient evidence of Donne's own text. In *A Funerall Elegie*, Donne's original poem on the death of Elizabeth Drury, there is certainly a difference in connotation between "she," referring to the dead girl, and "shee" who is symbolic of virtues. "*She's* demolish'd . . . / Must wee say *she's* dead? . . . *She* soone expir'd, / Cloath'd in her virgin white integritie." These are straightforward statements about a dead young virgin. Nature, however, is "shee":

> Thus brave and confident may Nature bee,
> Death cannot give her such another blow,
> Because *shee* cannot such another show.   (Lines 34–36)

And Donne rises from the particular dead girl to symbol and idea in such lines as these:

> But those fine spirits which do tune, and set
> This Organ, are those peeces which beget
> Wonder and love; and these were *shee;* and *shee*
> Being spent, the world must needs decrepit bee;
> For since death will proceed to triumph still,
> He can finde nothing, after her, to kill,
> Except the world it selfe, so great as *shee*.   (Lines 27–33)

In the *Anniversary Poems* Donne's deliberate distinction between "she" and "double shee" is, I am persuaded, an important clue through what has seemed a perplexed maze. "She," as I have said, is a real person, but only on rare occasions in either the *First* or *Second Anniversary* does the pronoun refer to Elizabeth Drury, who, as Donne's title pages indicate, was merely an "occasion" for the most profound poems he ever wrote.[8] References to the dead girl occur infrequently, usually at the beginning or the end of the poems. In

---

[8] Although we usually refer to the two poems as the *First Anniversary* and the *Second Anniversary*, these phrases were subtitles rather than titles to Donne himself. In the 1612 edition the phrases appear in small capitals, italicized, at the top of each title-page, immediately before the main title, which in the first poem is *An Anatomie of the World*, in the second, *Of The Progres of the Soule*. In the 1625 edition, the "anniversary" phrases appear only at the end of the long title. The full title of the first poem was: *An Anatomie of the World. Wherein, By Occasion Of the untimely death of Mistris Elizabeth Drury, the frailtie and the decay of this whole World is represented.* The title of the second was: *Of The Progres of the Soule. Wherein: By Occasion of The Religious Death of Mistris Elizabeth Drury, the incommodities of the Soule in this life, and her exaltation in the next, are Contemplated.*

these there is not more but rather less of the exaggeration and hyperbole that was customary among Renaissance writers of elegies.

I

The "she" who takes Elizabeth Drury's place implies a second level of meaning, as "shee" a third. But before I attempt identification of "she" and interpretation of "shee," I must indicate the central framework Donne used in both poems, which was much more familiar in his time than in ours. Donne's *Anniversaries* are as remarkable as *Lycidas* in their Renaissance art of mingling classical and Christian themes. Each of the three movements of *Lycidas* begins with a pagan convention; each ends with a Christian climax. "That strain I heard was of a higher mood," Milton tells us when at the end of the first section he returns to classical convention. "Return, Alpheus, the dread voice is past / That shrunk thy streams"—so after the lines on St. Peter, he returns again to the pagan, from which he rises again to the Christian in the third movement, with its climax in the vision of Paradise. Edward King's death was Milton's "occasion" as Elizabeth Drury's was Donne's; legitimately Milton memorialized the dead youth first as "shepherd-poet" in the classical tradition, then as "shepherd-priest," in the Christian tradition. The framework of the elegy, with its invocation, its lament of nature, its procession of mourners, its flower-passage, was as classical as the laments of Theocritus, Bion, or Virgil; yet always in *Lycidas* the "higher mood" of Christianity triumphs over paganism. So too in Donne's *Anniversaries;* yet the classical substratum is always there.

Beneath and behind Donne's companion-poems lay one

of the oldest classical tales, familiar from Hesiod to Virgil, so well known to Renaissance readers that Donne felt no more need of retelling it than did Milton when he referred to the same legend in his youthful poem on the death of a girl in infancy:

> Or wert thou that Just Maid who once before
> Forsook the hated earth, oh! tell me sooth,
> And camest again to visit us once more?

"In all *shee* did," Donne wrote in *The Second Anniversary*, "some Figure of the Golden Times was hid." That clue is fair enough, as is the statement: "She of whom th' Ancients seem'd to prophesie, / When they call'd vertues by the name of *shee*." Renaissance readers would have recognized the story of Astraea, goddess of Justice, the maiden who fled a wicked world to remain forever in heaven as the constellation Virgo.[9]

The decay of Nature and the degeneration of man, Donne's theme in the *Anniversaries*, had been as familiar in paganism as in Christianity, symbolized in the four ages of the world, the Golden Age, the Silver Age, the Bronze Age, and the Iron Age. "O Age of rusty Iron," Donne wrote in his fifth satire, echoing an old commonplace, the persistent cry of melancholy men who seem always to feel themselves living in the worst age of the world. From Hesiod onward, the story of degeneration had gathered to itself all manner of details describing the increasing evils of man. For our purposes, the account of the poet Aratus in his *Phaenomena* (translated by Cicero, quoted by St. Paul) may serve best, since in Aratus

---

[9] Hiram Haydn first suggested to me the significance of the Astraea legend in the *Anniversaries* in 1942 when he was working upon his doctoral dissertation at Columbia University, later published in *The Counter Renaissance* (New York, 1950). The fullest treatment of the Astraea legend may be found in Frances Yates, "Queen Elizabeth as Astraea," *Journal of the Warburg and Courtauld Institutes*, X (1947), 27–82.

as in Donne the old legend was adapted to cosmography. Aratus brought into a whole earlier fragmentary ethical and religious interpretations of the primitive story, and made the central figure in his account Astraea, the Maiden. Here he explains the origin of the constellation Virgo: [10]

And beneath both feet of Bootes behold the Maiden, who, in her hands bears the Ear of Corn gleaming. Whether she be of the race of Astraeus, who they say was the ancient father of the stars, or of another, may she be borne on in safety. Now another tale is current among men, to wit, how formerly she was on earth, and met men face to face, and neither disdained the tribe of ancient men nor women, but sat amid them, immortal though she was. And they called her Justice. . . . Not yet did men understand hateful war or vituperative disputes or din of battle, but they lived simply . . . and Justice herself, mistress of the people, giver of just things, furnished all things a thousand fold. This continued as long as the earth nourished the Golden Race.

The Silver Race succeeded to the Golden, a race, as Hesiod had said, "much worse by far, a race of silver, like the golden race neither in outward appearance nor in mind." Astraea no longer lived among men, though she had not yet left the world. She betook herself to the high places, and "came down from the echoing mountains only toward evening . . . assailing and threatening them because of their wickedness," warning them that, if the degeneration of man continued, she would never appear among them again. A third age came upon the world: "the Bronze Race was born, men more deadly than their predecessors, the first to forge the evil-

[10] A convenient summary of classical treatments of the theme of the Four Ages and of Astraea may be found in *A Documentary History of Primitivism and Related Ideas*, by Arthur O. Lovejoy and George Boas (Baltimore, 1935), Vol. I, chap. II. My quotations in this section are from their translations.

working sword. . . . Then Justice hated the race of men and flew to Heaven." The Iron Age succeeded to the Bronze, and man's wickedness was such as knew no bounds. Never since the Silver has the Maiden come down to man; only in the heavens do they still see her, the constellation Virgo, "the Maiden near to far-seen Bootes."

So the story passed from one generation to another, retold in many forms, yet always retaining its basic pattern of a degenerate world from which primitive virtues had fled. Of all the versions known to the Renaissance, Ovid's in the *Metamorphoses* was the most familiar; his was a pessimistic account of a world from which all virtues have disappeared forever, from which the Maiden has fled to the stars. Not until Virgil did a strain of optimism enter into the old theme. In the supposed "Messianic eclogue," Virgil used the familiar story, but weaving into its texture other matter from the prophetic writers, prophesied the ultimate return of Astraea in a future when the world's great age should begin anew. "The last age of the Cumean song has come; the great succession of the ages begins anew. Now the Maiden returns, and the reign of Saturn; now a new race is sent down from high heaven . . . Begin thy great career, dear child of the gods, Jove's mighty progeny; the time is now at hand."

As the Renaissance had inherited the legend from Ovid and from Virgil, they could find in it both the full flower of pessimism and the seeds of optimism. The older versions lie behind the melancholy of the *Anatomie:* "Shee is dead," "Shee is gone," and with her have gone justice and truth and beauty. At the end of the *Second Anniversary,* we hear the note of triumph: although "Shee" has left the world, Virgo still shines in the heavens, and another Virgin will "by Death survive All this in Heaven."

The Virgo legend was a fitting choice on Donne's part for the basic framework of an elegy taking its departure from the death of a young virgin, an elegy, too, into which he wished to pour his own melancholy over the state of a degenerate world. "Our age," as he said, "was Iron, and rustie too." Astraea had again left a world from which old values were vanishing. She had been a symbol of Justice, but where was justice now that "Reward and punishment are bent awry"? She had been a symbol of beauty, but beauty too was fled, now that "beauties best, proportion, is dead." She had been harmony and symmetry, but now

> Shee by whose lines proportion should bee
> Examin'd, measure of all Symmetree,
> Whom had that Ancient seen, who thought soules made
> Of Harmony, he would at next have said
> That Harmony was shee, and thence infer,
> That soules were but Resultances from her . . .
> Shee, after whom, what forme soe'r we see,
> Is discord, and rude incongruitie;
> Shee, shee is dead, shee's dead; when thou knowst this,
> Thou knowst how ugly a monster this world is.
>
> (*FA*, ll. 309–26)

No pagan poet more poignantly lamented the passing of Astraea from an ugly, base, and degenerate world than did the Christian Donne.

Long before Donne's time, Astraea, like many other pagan characters, had been kidnapped to Christianity. In the Middle Ages her story became involved with the allegory of the Four Daughters of God, which had developed from a Biblical verse: "Mercy and truth have met together; justice and peace have kissed." But while there was passing reminiscence of that allegory in Donne's lines,

> And she made peace, for no peace is like this,
> That beauty, and chastity together kisse,   (*SA*, ll. 363–64)

Donne's Christianizing of Astraea had less to do with medieval allegory than with Virgil's "Messianic eclogue." As
Christians read Virgil's compliment to an unborn child into
a prophecy of the coming of Christ, so they found in Astraea-
Virgo an anticipation of the Virgin Mary, as Donne suggests:

> She, of whom th' Ancients seem'd to prophesie,
> When they call'd vertues by the name of *shee*;
> Shee in whom vertue was so much refin'd,
> That for Allay unto so pure a minde
> She tooke the weaker Sex; shee that could drive
> The poysonous tincture, and the staine of Eve,
> Out of her thoughts and deeds; and purifie
> All, by a true religious Alchymie;
> Shee, shee is dead; shee's dead.   (*FA*, ll. 175–82)

Here "She" is Mary the woman; "*shee*" is Astraea; but the
generalized "Shee" of the refrain involves, I think, still another woman, as in many passages in both poems. It is not
Elizabeth Drury nor Astraea nor the Virgin Mary who is the
central character in the *Anniversary Poems*, but another Elizabeth, another Virgo, another Virgin, Elizabeth the Virgin
Queen.[11]

John Donne had not been among the poets who in 1603
joined in the chorus of lament for the dead queen. Indeed
only two years earlier he had been writing a long poem in
which Elizabeth was to have been the final villain of his piece.

---

[11] Basing his argument upon entirely different premises, Marius Bewley
also identifies "shee" with Queen Elizabeth in his "Religious Cynicism in
Donne's Poetry," *Kenyon Review*, XIV (1952), 619–46. Mr. Bewley believes that Donne is describing his apostasy from the Roman Catholic
Church. Louis Martz replies specifically to Mr. Bewley's and my identification in *The Poetry of Meditation*, Appendix 2, pp. 353–56.

In 1603 Donne was still a Roman Catholic, and no matter how thoroughly a Catholic might respect Elizabeth the State, he must inevitably deny Elizabeth the Church. But much had happened in Donne's personal life, as much had happened in the little world of England. In 1611 and 1612 Donne wrote the "epicedes and obsequies" upon the queen which he had refused to write in 1603. The *Anniversary Poems,* I am persuaded, constitute the greatest poetic tribute to Elizabeth after *The Faerie Queene.*

So far as Elizabeth Drury was concerned, Donne had said all that he could say in *A Funerall Elegie.* When he returned to his theme on the occasion of the first anniversary of her death, he paid Sir Robert Drury the compliment of using his dead daughter as his point of departure for a poem upon the greater Elizabeth, for whom the young girl had been named. Read against the background of the tributes written in the great days when Elizabeth was at the height of her glory and the outpouring of poetry at the time of her virtual apotheosis in death, the *Anniversaries* take on very different meaning and proportion. At least from the time of the Armada, as we know, Elizabeth had been glorified as a symbol. Into her had been read far more hyperbole than we find in the *Anniversaries.*[12] She was Diana and Cynthia, Laura, Gloriana, Belphoebe, and a host of other mythological and idyllic characters. All the themes I have suggested in Donne's "shee" had been found in her. She was often "Earth's true Astraea,"

---

[12] Many of the contemporary tributes to Elizabeth have been collected by Elkin Calhoun Wilson in *England's Eliza* (Harvard University Press, 1939). I have borrowed from Mr. Wilson the lines below on "Virgo" (Richard Barnfield, *Cynthia,* 1595) and the Dekker quotation. Mr. Wilson treats at length the development in England of "Virgin" idolatry. In his chapter on "The Ladie of the Sea" are many interesting parallels for Donne's passage on the queen "whose rich eyes and brest Guilt the West Indies, and perfum'd the East," which I discuss below.

who had brought back the Age of Gold, as in the conclusion to *Histriomastix,* and throughout Sir John Davies's acrostic *Hymnes to Astraea:*

> But whereto shall we bend our layes?
> Even up to Heaven, againe to raise
> The Mayd, which thence descended,
> Hath brought againe the golden dayes,
> And all the world amended.

She was "Elizabetha Virgo,"

> Then since an heavenly Name doth thee befall,
> Thou VIRGO art (if any signe at all).

She was the Virgin, *par excellence.* "Her life (which was dedicated to Virginitie)" Dekker wrote in *The Wonderfull Yeare,* "both beginning and closing up a miraculous Mayden circle; for she was borne upon a Lady Eve, and died upon a Lady Eve." Elizabeth the Virgin had been sung with the fervor of both knights of chivalry and troubadours. Idolatry such as Catholics felt for the Virgin Mary was hers, for to her jealous subjects she, like Mary, was both their "Maiden Queene" and their "Virgin Mother,"—as woman unstained, as monarch mystically married to England. All this is familiar enough to any reader of Elizabethan poetry; all this was Donne's poetic heritage when at last he turned to praise the queen he had once condemned as a heretic.

If we read the *Anniversary Poems* with Queen Elizabeth rather than Elizabeth Drury in mind, we shall see how familiar are many of Donne's supposed "hyperboles." Other poets had been more excessive in their praise of Elizabeth's physical beauty than Donne, who was more concerned with her soul than her body:

> She, of whose soule, if wee may say, 'twas Gold,
> Her body was th' Electrum, and did hold
> Many degrees of that; wee understood
> Her by her sight; her pure, and eloquent blood
> Spoke in her cheekes, and so distinctly wrought,
> That one might almost say, her body thought;
> Shee, shee, thus richly and largely hous'd, is gone.
>
> *(SA,* ll. 241–47)

Earlier poets had exaggerated Elizabeth's learning more grossly than did Donne, who again was concerned less with intellectual attainments than with virtue:

> Shee who all libraries had thoroughly read
> At home in her owne thoughts, and practised
> So much good as would make as many more: . . .
> She who in th' art of knowing Heaven, was growne
> Here upon earth, to such perfection,
> That she hath, ever since to Heaven she came,
> (In a far fairer print,) but read the same:
> Shee, shee not satisfied with all this waight,
> (For so much knowledge, as would over-fraight
> Another, did but ballast her) is gone
> As well t' enjoy, as get perfection.
> And cals us after her, in that shee tooke,
> (Taking her selfe) our best, and worthiest booke.
>
> *(SA,* ll. 303–20)

But let us go back to the *First Anniversary* to see that from the beginning Donne is talking not of a dead girl but of a dead monarch:

> When that Queene ended here her progresse time,
> And, as t'her standing house to heaven did climbe,
> Where, loath to make the Saints attend her long,
> She's now a part both of the Quire, and Song,

> This World, in that great earthquake, languished;
> For in a common bath of teares it bled. . . . (*FA*, ll. 7-12)

Certainly this seems legitimate language about the death of Elizabeth, when we remember the dread with which many of her subjects faced an uncertain future, realizing that her death marked the end of an epoch. Both symbolically and in reality Elizabeth for many years had held together a commonwealth that socially and economically was beginning to crumble:

> So mankinde feeling now a generall thaw,
> A strong example gone, equall to law,
> The Cyment which did faithfully compact
> And glue all vertues, now resolv'd and slack'd . . .
> Sicke World, yea, dead, yea putrified, since shee
> Thy intrinsique balme, and thy preservative,
> Can never be renew'd . . .   (*FA*, ll. 47-58)

Elizabeth's death had seemed indeed the end of the world— the end of a world that England was not to know again. "Her death hath taught us dearely that thou art / Corrupt and mortall in thy purest part." For all his radicalism in poetry —if, indeed he was a poetic radical—Donne was a traditionalist in his feeling for a stable world in which the old values had seemed to exist. " 'Tis all in peeces, all cohaerence gone, / All just supply and all relation." "Shee, shee is gone; shee's gone," and with her have gone beauty, harmony, proportion, justice and truth, the absolutes of a departing world.

The "new Philosophy" was not Donne's main theme in the *First Anniversary*, though we have so isolated the passage from its context that it seems to be. The "new Philosophy" was only a final straw; the camel's back was already broken. More subjectively—and with much more reason—than Shake-

speare in *Troilus and Cressida*, Donne felt in the chaos in the
macrocosm one more indication of chaos in the microcosm,
the confused political and economic "little kingdom" of England, in which "Prince, Subject, Father, Sonne, are things
forgot." "Order," established and maintained by Elizabeth,
was gone; traditional values of royalty, aristocracy, family
were facing disruption. The individual was no longer content
to play his allotted role in an established scheme,

> For every man alone thinkes he has got
> To be a Phoenix, and that then can bee
> None of that kinde, of which he is, but hee. (*FA*, ll. 216–18)

"This is the worlds condition now"—now that "shee" is gone.
Many of the epithets that follow are familiar compliments to
the Queen, the kind of epithets showered upon her as,
through her mariners, she became a monarch to whom both
East and West paid tribute:

> she whose rich eyes and brest
> Guilt the West Indies, and perfum'd the East;
> Whose having breath'd in this world, did bestow
> Spice on these Iles, and bad them still smell so.
> And that rich Indie, which doth gold interre,
> Is but as single money, coyn'd from her.   (*FA*, ll. 229–34)

In his first encomium on the Queen, Donne's imagination
had found analogies in such alchemical terms as "balme" and
"preservative." Here, with the "new Philosophy" in mind,
he drew his figures from the greatest English discovery of the
"new science." Shortly before Her Majesty's death, William
Gilbert had published his *De Magnete*, in which he had shown
that the earth was a great magnet, exerting a "magnetick
vigour" without which the world would go to pieces. In
Donne's poem Elizabeth was both the magnetic compass

guiding men who "did in their voyage in this worlds Sea stray," and the magnetic force that had held her world together. But now

> She that should all parts to reunion bow,
> She that had all Magnetique force alone,
> To draw and fasten sundred parts in one; . . .
> Shee, shee is dead; shee's dead.   (*FA*, ll. 220–28)

Throughout the *First Anniversary*—the subject of which is the world—Donne wrote of Elizabeth in the little world of England which she had cemented so firmly, in which she had upheld "order" and those verities central to Donne's ethics and aesthetics, symmetry, proportion, harmony. The old world was gone, since "Shee which did inanimate and fill / The world" was gone. "In this last long night" only a glimmering light was left; yet still "the twilight of her memory doth stay."

Donne might have written some parts of his tribute to Elizabeth even in 1603, since, in common with most of her subjects, he had always respected Elizabeth the State. The lament would not have been so poignant, for the years that had passed had served to make him more aware of what England had lost in the way of stability. But Donne could not possibly have written the climactic sections of the *Second Anniversary* in 1603. As in the second poem, he passed from the death of the body to the life of the spirit, from mortality to immortality, from the world to Heaven, so he passed from Elizabeth the State to Elizabeth the Church.

Donne's own title for the second poem was not the *Second Anniversary* but *Of the Progres of the Soule*. Shortly before the Queen's death, as I have said, he had been writing another *Progresse of the Soule*, his most ambitious satire,

which, unfortunately from his later point of view, had circulated in manuscript. An elaborate study in metempsychosis, it
attempted to treat the passage of a soul from the vegetable,
through the animal, to the human kingdom, and by so doing
to condemn, from a Catholic point of view, the progress of
heresy. Ben Jonson described the design thus:

The conceit . . . was that he sought the soule of that apple
which Eve pulled and thereafter made it the soule of a bitch, then
a shee wolf, and so of a woman; his generall purpose was to have
brought in all the bodies of the Hereticks from the soul of Cain,
and at last left in the bodie of Calvin. Of this he never wrotte but
one sheet, and now, since he was made Doctor, repenteth highlie
and seeketh to destroy all his poems.

But Donne himself intended his satire to go beyond Calvin.
The final destination of the soul of heresy was to have been
in Elizabeth, head of the anti-Roman Church:

> For the great soule which here amongst us now
> Doth dwell, and moves that hand, and tongue, and brow,
> Which, as the Moone the sea, moves us; to heare
> Whose story, with long patience you will long;
> (For 'tis the crowne, and last straine of my song)
> This soule to whom Luther, and Mahomet were
> Prisons of flesh; this soule which oft did teare,
> And mend the wracks of th' Empire, and late Rome,
> And liv'd when every great change did come,
>   Had first in paradise, a low, but fatall roome.
>   (*Progresse of the Soule*, VII)

So the Queen had seemed to the young Catholic satirist in
1601. Whatever her virtues as monarch, he not only denied
her supremacy as head of a church, but relegated her to a
group of women against whom he frequently directed his
satire. By 1611 Donne's attitude toward women had changed,

in part because of his marriage to Ann More whom he both loved and respected, in part because he had come into closer contact with a group of women to whom he addressed many of his verse-epistles—women such as Magdalen Herbert, the Countess of Huntingdon, the Countess of Bedford—all of whom he had reason to admire. More important, he had left the Roman Church, and within a short time after he wrote the *Anniversaries* was to be ordained a priest of the Anglican Church. The *Second Anniversary* was at once his supreme tribute to Elizabeth and his *apologia*.

At the end of the new *Progres of the Soule*, deliberately intended to take the place of the earlier *Progresse of the Soule*, Donne made his public confession of faith. In the great diapason he brought together all his themes:

> Up, up, my drowsie Soule, where thy new eare
> Shall in the Angels songs no discord heare. (*SA*, ll. 339–40)

As his soul mounted on its journey, Donne again remembered the Virgin Mary:

> Where thou shalt see the blessed Mother-maid
> Joy in not being that, which men have said.
> Where she is exalted more for being good,
> Then for her interest of Mother-hood. (*SA*, ll. 341–44)

But the vision of Mary was not a climax of his journey. Circle by circle his soul, like Dante's, ascended to Paradise through the solemn troops and sweet societies of the Patriarchs, who anticipated the coming of Christ, the Prophets who saw their prophecies come true, the Apostles who preached Christ, the Martyrs who died for Him. In his early satire Donne had said that Elizabeth the Heretic "had in Paradise a low and fatall room." Now in the highest circle of all, among the Virgins closest to the Holy Ghost, he found the Virgin Queen, whom he acknowledged as the Head of the True Church. "She" and "Shee," the woman and the symbol, are interwoven in his vision:

> Up, up, for in that squadron there doth live
> She, who hath carried thither new degrees
> (As to their number) to their dignities.
> Shee, who being to her selfe a State, injoy'd
> All royalties which any State employ'd.   (*SA*, ll. 356–60)

Looking back, he realized that actions he had once considered merely political had been truly religious:

> For shee made warres, and triumph'd; reason still
> Did not o'rthrow, but rectifie her will;
> And she made peace, for no peace is like this,
> That beauty, and chastity together kisse:
> She did high justice, for she crucified
> Every first motion of rebellious pride:
> And she gave pardons, and was liberall,
> For, onely her selfe except, she pardon'd all.
>
> (*SA*, ll. 361–68)

State and Church have met in her: Elizabeth the Church, whom he had long denied, he gladly acknowledges:

> As these prerogatives being met in one,
> Made her a soveraigne State; *religion*
> *Made her a Church;* and these two made her all.
> She who was all this All, and could not fall
> To worse, by company (for she was still
> More Antidote, then all the world was ill,)
> Shee, shee doth leave it, and by Death, survive
> All this, in Heaven.[13]   (*SA*, ll. 373–80)

Lament and despair are changed to victory; the conclusion is the triumph of immortality and the faith of a believer in the true Church, and in the "last great Consummation." "Shee,"

---

[13] The italics in this passage are mine.

that symbol and complex of many symbols, is not dead. "Shee" of whom the world was not worthy has left it, like Astraea, but like Virgo she remains eternally in the heavens, "Shee, shee doth leave it, and by Death survive / All this, in Heaven." Elizabeth was the Proclamation; John Donne's is to be the Voice calling men to what he now acknowledges as the True Church.

In his "double shee" Donne combined memories of the pagan Virgo, the Virgin Mary, and the Virgin Queen, all woven into his "Idea of a Woman," symbol of beauty, virtue, justice, truth. It is "Shee" who merits those encomiums critics have attempted to heap upon a dead young girl. Read in their context, the *Anniversaries* are far from being "preposterous eulogies" filled with "execrable extravagancies," "prophane and full of blasphemies." They are the lament of a great poet over the decay of a world from which all values seemed to have fled, a Christian's confession of faith in immortality and the Resurrection, and a prophet's vision of another Age of Gold when "Shee," who was truth and beauty, justice and righteousness, mercy and peace, would be found again, not on earth but in Heaven.

II

John Donne had seen the death of a world in the death of Elizabeth; but he was to be present at the death of the world in a quite different sense. One Circle of Perfection— the "order" and "proportion" that had given form to the microcosm of England—had broken; but other circles were to be shattered in both the geocosm and the macrocosm. Donne proved a prophet in more senses thàn one. Earlier than any other English poet he realized the extent to which "new

Philosophy" might call all in doubt, and the breaking up of order in the world scheme might prove a poignant parallel for the breaking up of order in the state. Let us return to the *First Anniversary* from another point of view.

The theme of the *First Anniversary* and of the first part of the *Second* is decay—a persistent motif for a generation obsessed with physical aspects of death. Hamlet with his brooding upon skulls, Claudio with his

> to die, and go we know not where;
> To lie in cold obstruction, and to rot,

were no more morbid on the subject than was Sir Thomas Browne who, as physician, was only too familiar with decay and death, yet who prefaced one of his sombre disquisitions with the words, "I am not so much afraid of Death, as ashamed of it." Even in his early poems Donne had reflected the combined repulsion and attraction of physiological details of the body which he proposed to "anatomize" in one of the many "anatomies" of a period when dissection had gone farther than ever before on the part of physicians, and when laymen, with fear and fascination, watched or read of new discoveries science was making in the little world of man.

But the theme of the *Anatomie* is not only the death of man. Its subtitle reads: "Wherein, by Occasion of the Untimely Death of Mistress Elizabeth Drury, *the Frailty and the Decay of this whole World is Represented*." Man was sick, and the world was sick; the illness of one world was reflected in the other. Both man and his world were approaching their end.[14] To the seventeenth century, laments over the old age and sickness of the world were not rhetoric but fact,

[14] Several of the themes I have treated in this section are developed in *Mountain Gloom and Mountain Glory*, to which I have referred in the Preface.

authority for which lay in the Bible. Shakespeare's Rosalind said, "The poor world is almost six thousand years old," but John Donne could have dated the birth of the world exactly. The chronology of the world has always fascinated mankind, though during the Christian era, chronologies had almost forgotten the sense of the sweep of time suggested by the Greeks, and completely lost the oriental idea of even vaster stages of unrecorded time. God had created the world in six days; on the seventh He rested. By the kind of analogical thinking with which we have become familiar, Augustine had made old traditions into a system which taught that both the world and man would proceed through seven stages. The life of the world would be six ages; the seventh would be the millennium, the peace of God after the destruction of the globe. If the Christian Fathers did not always agree with the Jewish Doctors in accepting the date of the original Creation as 3761 B.C., their corrections were only a matter of years. I shall follow the chronology of the great Reformation "Father," Martin Luther, in part because it was of great influence in Protestant countries, in part because Luther conveniently used round numbers, easy to remember, but largely because Luther's interpretation of the history of man and of the world was as pessimistic as anything in Donne's *Anniversary Poems*.

Like most chronologists, Luther based his *Supputatio Annorum Mundi* upon the old *Elia Propheta*:

> Sex milibus annorum stabit Mundus,
>   Duobus milibus inane.
>   Duobus Milibus Lex.
>   Duobus milibus Messiah.
> Isti sunt Sex dies hebdomadae coram Dei. Septimus
>   Dies Sabbatum aeternum est.

"The world's history," Luther wrote in his *Conversations*, "I divide into six ages, the ages of Adam, Noah, Abraham, David, Christ, and the Pope. . . . But the Pope will not complete his millennium." One of the most melancholy of chronologists, Luther read into the lesson taught by the past an unbroken history of what may be called "degenerative cycles" of man and of the world, which was created in 4000 B.C. Each "great age" of two thousand years had begun well; during each period steady degeneration occurred in both man and the world. The first "great age" that began in the Garden of Eden degenerated until, with the generation of Enoch, mankind had become so evil that God wiped out all men but the family of Noah, and by the Deluge changed even the contour of the globe. The second age started at a higher level than that to which the first had fallen, though inevitably at a lower level than the age of Adam. But again degeneration occurred until at the end of the era, four thousand years after Creation, humanity had reached a nadir. The world's great age began anew with the coming of Christ, sent by a merciful God to save even the worst of sinners, but again man had shown steady degeneration. Living in the last age of the world, Luther was persuaded that a just God would not permit that world to fulfill the course He had once ordained. The pope would not complete his millennium. In his *Table Talk* he once dated the probable destruction of the world as early as 1560. "It is my firm belief," he wrote, "that the angels are getting ready, putting on their armor, and girding their swords about them, for the last day is already breaking. . . . The world will perish shortly."

The world that began so auspiciously in 4000 B.C., if permitted to run its original course of six thousand years, must perish no later than A.D. 2000. We who live in the twilight of the world should understand better than any other generation the impotence of an earlier age when even learned men believed that the Final Catastrophe was close upon them. Our ancestors of the seventeenth century after Christ were uncomfortably near the day when

> The cloud-capp'd towers, the gorgeous palaces,
> The solemn temples, the great globe itself,
> Yea all which it inherit, shall dissolve.

Behind them the syllables of recorded time spoke man's decay for more than fifty-five centuries; before them stretched only years, perhaps only days. No wonder that they were obsessed by Time, still finite in their imaginations, having its beginning with Adam, its end perhaps with themselves. Crashaw wrote *Upon the Frontispiece of Mr. Isaacson's Chronologie:*

> History reares her Pyramids, more tall
> Then were th' Aegyptians. . . .
> On these she lifts the World, and on their base
> Shewes the two terms and limits of Time's race:
> That, the Creation is; the Judgement this;
> That, the World's Morning; this, her Midnight is.

"Had we but World enough, and Time." World enough they had, for during their own Renaissance period their fathers had made the hemisphere into a sphere, had discovered the far-flung regions of a globe which ironically was growing to its greatest extent just before its death, as Phineas Fletcher suggested in *The Purple Island:*

> Vain men, too fondly wise, who plough the seas,
> With dangerous pains another world to finde;
> Adding new worlds to th' old, and scorning ease,
> The worlds vast limits dayly more unbinde.

> The agéd world, though now it falling shows,
> And hastes to set, yet still in dying grows.   (1.36)

But Time they lacked. Their first minute, after noon, was night, for at their backs they seemed to hear Time's winged chariot hurrying near.

Even in Donne's time there were those who denied that the world was wearing out, that it was growing old and must perish of disease and age. Men like George Hakewill [15] insisted that nothing in the nature of the world led to degeneration and decay; Nature operated upon orderly laws. Yet even the Hakewills of the earlier seventeenth century, living under the shadow of the prophetic writers and chronologists, agreed that the world would perish, though not of itself, because of the Fiat of God. Sir Thomas Browne expressed their point of view in the *Religio Medici:* "I believe the World grows near its end, yet it is neither old nor decayed, nor shall ever perish upon the ruines of its own Principles. As the work of Creation was above Nature, so is its adversary, annihilation; without which the World hath not its end, but its mutation. Now what force should be able to consume it thus far, without the breath of God, which is the truest consuming flame, my Philosophy cannot inform me." [16] But the nature of the world was at best an academic question to men who faced its death. For all his scientific optimism and his insistence that man study the Book of God's Works, Browne believed even more fully in the Book of God's Words, as it had been interpreted for generations. In the *Urne-Buriall* he wrote the epitaph of a generation without a future:

---

[15] Hakewill's position is discussed by R. F. Jones in *Ancients and Moderns* (St. Louis, 1936), and by Victor Harris in *All Coherence Gone* (Chicago, 1949).

[16] *Religio Medici*, 1.45 (Keynes ed. p. 56).

'Tis too late to be ambitious. The great mutations of the world are acted, or time may be too short for our designes. To extent our Memories by Monuments, whose death we dayly pray for, and whose duration we cannot hope, without injury to our expectations, in the advent of the last day, were a contradiction to our beliefs. We whose generations are ordained in the setting part of time, are providentally taken off from such imaginations. And being necessitated to eye the remaining particle of futurity, are naturally constituted unto thoughts of the next world, and cannot excusably decline the consideration of that duration, which maketh Pyramids pillars of snow, and all that's past a moment.[17]

As Milton's Adam saw the vision of the sad future he was bringing upon mankind, so Donne, looking back, read the world's history. "In Adam's Fall we sinnéd all"; we have left undone those things we ought to have done, and we have done those things we ought not to have done, and there is no health in us. This is the opening strain of the *Anatomie:*

> There is no health; Physitians say that wee,
> At best, enjoy but a neutralitie.
> And can there bee worse sicknesse, then to know
> That we are never well, nor can be so?   (*FA*, ll. 91–94)

Adam, for all his sins, had lived to the age of nine hundred and ninety-nine; some of his descendants lived for a thousand years. But

> Where is this mankinde now? who lives to age,
> Fit to be made Methusalem his page?   (*FA*, ll. 128–29)

"And as in lasting, so in length is man, / Contracted to an inch, who was a spanne." There were giants in those days, but now "mankinde decays to soone, / We are scarce our Fathers shadowes cast at noone." "And as our bodies, so our mindes are crampt."

---

[17] *Hydriotaphia*, v (Keynes ed., IV, 45).

Wee seeme ambitious, Gods whole worke t' undoe;
Of nothing hee made us, and we strive too,
To bring our selves to nothing backe.   (*FA*, ll. 155–57)

All this was literary and theological commonplace, familiar in Hebraic and Christian teaching. Donne had merely adapted to his own idiom what the Fathers had said for centuries. This section on the decay of man needs no gloss. We too have inherited these ideas from sermons or the Mass, from confession manuals or the Book of Common Prayer, or from the poets. But as Donne goes on to treat "the Decay of Nature in other parts," he enters upon territory less familiar to us after three centuries of modern science. Decay and death are not limited to man; through man's sin they have passed to the globe. The microcosm has affected the geocosm. As Vaughan said,

[Man] drew the Curse upon the world, and Crackt
The whole frame with his fall.

When Milton's Eve ate the apple, "Earth felt the wound, and Nature from her seat / Sighing through all her works, gave signs of woe." When Adam ate, "Earth trembled from her entrails, as again / In pangs, and Nature gave a second groan." Donne follows this tradition of the changes that occurred in Nature, but he goes further, introducing an idea which Milton implicitly denied. The most spectacular change in external nature is in the contour of the whole globe, which is no longer the perfect sphere, a copy of the spherical universe, that emerged from the waters at the voice of God:

But keepes the earth her round proportion still?
Doth not a Tenarif, or higher Hill
Rise so high like a Rocke, that one might thinke
The floating Moone would shipwracke there, and sinke?

Seas are so deepe, that Whales being strooke to day,
Perchance to morrow, scarse at middle way
Of their wish'd journies end, the bottome, die.
And men, to sound depths, so much line untie,
As one might justly thinke, that there would rise
At end thereof, one of th' Antipodies. . . .
Then solidnesse, and roundnesse have no place.
Are these but warts, and pock-holes in the face
Of th' earth? Thinke so; but yet confesse, in this
The worlds proportion disfigured is.   (*FA*, ll. 285–302)

Donne was writing of an old theological belief which we have long forgotten. When at the word of God the earth emerged, its surface was not irregular as we see it now, with mountains, the "warts of earth" as many called them, and profound depths, the "pock-holes." At the Creation the globe of earth was a true sphere, unmarked by the blemishes of height and depth, smooth, equal, even. In his mood of melancholy Donne went back to the old tradition of a smooth, unblemished, primitive earth, the perfect sphere of the Great Geometer. The gross irregularities of earth's surface, with its warts and pock-holes, were abiding evidence of the sin of man. The geocosm had been persistently affected by the microcosm. With each of man's major sins, the earth had grown increasingly ugly. Let man beat his breast, as he looked at Nature, and cry, "Mea Culpa! Mea maxima culpa!"

The once perfect sphere has suffered deformity. "Confesse, in this / The worlds proportion disfigured is." As always, disturbances in the larger world have been reflected in the "little commonwealth of man," for

Those two legges whereon it did rely,
Reward and punishment are bent awry.   (*FA*, ll. 303–4)

"Shee by whose lines proportion should bee / Examin'd, measure of all Symmetree," has left a world which has grown too ugly for her to bear,

> Shee, after whom, what forme soe'r we see,
> Is discord and rude incongruitie;
> Shee, shee is dead, shee's dead; when thou knowst this,
> Thou knowst how ugly a monster this world is.
>
> (*FA*, ll. 323–26)

The second of Donne's circles has broken; the once perfect sphere is cracked and awry. The world is not only old and sick but deformed. But weak and "inform" as it was it still seemed to live, "For theres a kinde of World remaining still." Not yet did the generation of Donne realize that they had been present at the death of the world.

III

And yet they had had warning enough not only in the "signes, tokens, and symptomes" of the astrologers but from the astronomers themselves. The first challenge had seemed only a still small voice.[18] The Copernican hypothesis disturbed man little, indeed disturbed the layman not at all. Could he not *see* that the sun still rose and set, and *feel* the earth as firm beneath his feet as it had been beneath Adam's? Poets poked satirical fun at

> Those clerks that think—think how absurd a jest!
> That neither heavens nor stars do turn at all
> Nor dance around this great, round, earthly ball,

---

[18] Since the publication of the first edition of this volume, my early papers on the development of the new astronomy (referred to on page 98, n. 14) have been republished in *Science and Imagination* ("Great Seal Books"; Ithaca, Cornell University Press, 1956).

> But the earth itself, this massy globe of our's
> Turns round about once every twice twelve hours! [19]

or, like Sir John Davies, laughingly proposed a new derivation for its name:

> Behold the World, how it is whirled round,
> And for it is so whirl'd, is named so.   (*Orchestra*, XXXIV)

Donne's early attitude had been entirely characteristic. In spite of his avid interest in novelty, he made almost no use of new astronomical theory in his youthful poetry. His first serious reference, in a letter to Sir Henry Goodyer about 1609, was a passing reflection, characteristically phrased in terms of the circle:

I often compare not you and me, but the sphear in which your resolutions are and my wheel, both I hope concentrique to God: for me thinks the new astronomy is thus appliable well, that we which are a little earth, should rather move towards God, than that He which is fulfilling, and can come no whither, should move towards us.

Even in *Ignatius His Conclave*, written only the year before he began the *Anniversary Poems*, his attitude toward Copernicanism was still only amused intellectual interest, as he haled Copernicus before the Judge of Hell, with Machiavelli and Paracelsus, as one of those "innovators" who had upset the world.

A louder warning to man had sounded in 1572, the supposed year of Donne's birth, when the first *nova* was observed in the heavens. "List, ye may hear great Aaron's bell." The ominous tone had been deeper and more resonant as men

---

[19] *The Divine Weeks of Josuah Sylvester, mainly tr. from the French of William de Saluste, lord of the Bartas*, IV.144–48. Ed. by Theron Wilber Haight (Waukesha, Wis., 1908).

watched the "new star" of 1604, which Donne remembered
well. Yet at first it afforded him only novel figures of speech:

> We have added to the world Virginia, and sent
> Two new starres lately to the firmament,

he wrote to the Countess of Bedford, as in his *Epithalamium*
on the marriage of Princess Elizabeth he found a new kind
of compliment:

> Be thou a new starre, that to us portends
> Ends of much wonder; And be Thou those ends.

Nevertheless Donne realized, as did every thoughtful man of
the period, that there was something startling about the appearance of "new stars"—more important to man than had
been the Copernican theory, though he was not yet aware
that a *nova* presaged the beginning of the end of a world and
of a universe.

"I know that all beneath the Moon decays," said Drummond. "Whatsoever is under the Moon," wrote Burton, "is
subject to corruption, alteration; and, so long as thou livest
upon the earth, look not for other." Joshuah Sylvester developed the theme further in *A Funerall Elegie:*

> All, that in this wide World is inclos'd,
> Is of Two kinds (and divers, too) compos'd:
> Mortall, the one; Immortall, th' other sort
> Exempt from Death. . . .
> > For all, above bright Cynthia's silver Car,
> Live out of fear, from Death and danger far:
> Far from corruption, and as free from change, . . .
> > And all, beneath her many-forméd flame,
> That sojourns here amid this fickle Frame . . .
> All, all doe dye.

Whether to Aristotle, to Augustine and Dante, or to Shake-speare, change and decay had always been limited to matter lying beneath the orb of the moon. The heavens, the handi-work of God, were eternal and immutable. As God had placed the stars in their constellations, so they had remained, an abiding proof to man that there was something unchange-able and permanent in the universe. Upon such celestial meta-physics, he had built his aesthetics and the ethics of an eternal and immutable morality. In youth Donne had had no reason to doubt the old belief. He wrote *To his Mistress, Suffering from Feaver,*

> These burning fits but meteors bee,
>> Whose matter in thee is soone spent,
> Thy beauty, and all parts, which are thee,
>> Are unchangeable firmament.

Aristotle had affirmed that there could be no new appear-ance in the heavens. Christians acknowledged only one "new star"—the one that appeared at the birth of Christ. Milton's Mary, in *Paradise Regained,* told Jesus of that wonder:

> A star, not seen before, in heaven appearing,
> Guided the wise men thither from the East. . . .
> By whose bright course, led on they found the place,
> Affirming it thy star, new-graven in heaven.   (1.249–53)

Donne wrote to the Countess of Huntingdon:

> Who vagrant transitory Comets sees,
> Wonders, because they are rare; But a new starre
> Whose motion with the firmament agrees,
> Is miracle; for, there no new things are.

But what of the star of 1572 in Cassiopeia? And what of the star of 1604 in Serpentarius? They were new stars, and there-

fore miracle—and many a believer waited for the Second
Coming of Christ. But to others of the Reformation generation, as pessimistic as Luther, the new stars were rather por-
tents, dire omens of God's wrath against a sinful generation,
presages to men that the angels were indeed making ready
their armor. God in His justice would not permit the world
to run its allotted course of six thousand years, but would destroy it by flood or fire. The end of the world was at hand.

The sound heard in 1610, with the publication of Galileo's
Sidereus Nuncius, was less Aaron's bell than the first note of
Gabriel's trumpet. In more senses than one Galileo had seen
through heaven and found no Heavenly City, but instead
"stars innumerable" never seen by human eye, the true nature
of the Milky Way, a new moon, possibly a new world in that
moon, and four new "planets," which though they proved
not planets but satellites of Jupiter, were to be as effectual as
new planets in destroying not only the old astronomy, but—
what mattered more to man—the very basis of the old astrology. Ancient philosophers had guessed at another universe than that man had always seen; Copernicus had proposed an hypothesis of another kind of universe; but Galileo
saw it with his eyes. Now for the first time a "new astronomy"
of new stars, new planets, a new moon, a new universe came
home to men's business and bosoms. Man decays: that had
long been a tenet of Christian faith. The world decays: that
too was orthodox enough. But beyond the orb of the moon,
there had been no decay, no change, no alteration. Yet the
new stars were in the celestial region and Galileo's telescope
had discovered spots on the moon, and, darker spots on the
sun. "When we look for incorruption in the heavens," wrote
Sir Thomas Browne, "we finde they are but like the Earth:
Durable in their main bodies, alterable in their parts; whereof

besides Comets and new stars, perspectives begin to tell tales.
And the spots that wander about the Sun, with Phaeton's
favour, would make clear conviction." [20] Drummond, like
many others, saw in the new discoveries omens of the end of
the world:

> New worlds seen, shine
> With other suns and moons, false stars decline,
> And dive in seas; red comets warn the air,
> And blaze, as other worlds were judged there.[21]

"And new Philosophy calls all in doubt," said Donne. Not
alone man and his world were threatened. Corruption, which
had spread by infection from man to his world, had now at-
tacked his universe. Nothing permanent and eternal remained:

> The Sun is lost, and th' earth, and no mans wit
> Can well direct him where to looke for it.
> And freely men confesse that this world's spent,
> When in the Planets, and the Firmament
> They seeke so many new: then see that this
> Is crumbled out againe to his Atomies;
> 'Tis all in peeces, all cohaerence gone;
> All just supply, and all Relation: (*FA*, ll. 207–14)

Most of all, to Donne the poet, the "new Philosophy" had
given the death-blow to that beauty which was symmetry,
proportion, harmony. One circle had broken with the breaking of the smooth sphere of the world; yet the greater circles
had remained, the perfect celestial spheres of the Great Geometer, in which man had seen the ultimate beauty of perfect
proportion:

[20] *Hydriotaphia*, v (Keynes ed., IV, 48).
[21] *The Shadow of the Judgement* in *Poems*, ed. by W. C. Ward (2 vols.;
London, n.d. [1894]), II, 61.

We thinke the heavens enjoy their Sphericall,
Their round proportion embracing all.   (*FA*, ll. 251–52)

Yet, as Donne came to realize, even the old astronomy, attempting to plot the "various and perplexed course" of the heavenly bodies, had found out

so many Eccentrique parts,
Such divers downe-right lines, such overthwarts,
As disproportion that pure forme.   (*FA*, ll. 255–57)

For centuries astronomers had attempted to explain the inequalities in the apparent motion of the sun: all that their theories proved was that

his course is not round; nor can the Sunne
Perfit a Circle, or maintaine his way
One inch direct; but where he rose to-day
He comes no more, but with a couzening line,
Steales by that point, and so is Serpentine.   (*FA*, ll. 268–72)

The planets that had originally kept their motions in the great cosmic dance had broken their pattern:

So, of the Starres which boast that they doe runne
In Circle still, none ends where he begun.
All their proportion's lame, it sinkes, it swels.
For of Meridians, and Parallels,
Man hath weav'd out a net, and this net throwne
Upon the Heavens, and now they are his owne.
                            (*FA*, ll. 275–80)

Old and new astronomers alike had "disproportioned that pure forme" of the heavens. One was as unintelligible as the other; only in one thing did they agree: "And, Oh, it can no more be questioned, / That beauties best, proportion, is dead."

Beauty was dead; proportion and symmetry had disappeared. The Circle of Perfection was gone from the heavens. Not only the world, but the whole universe suffered corruption. As man decayed and the world decayed, the universe too was dying. The old animate world, of which man was a living part, as it in turn was part of a living universe, was at its end. And indeed it was. To a greater extent than he realized, John Donne was present at the death of a world. Gabriel's trumpet had sounded. *Sex milibus annorum stabit Mundus*, declared *Elia Propheta*. Luther and many other chronologists had predicted that the last thousand years would not be completed; the world would end before its appointed time. Luther and the chronologists were right. The world created four thousand years before the birth of Christ did perish seventeen centuries after that event. The world of Aristotle, of Ptolemy, of Augustine and Dante, of Shakespeare, was gone. In its place was only a lesser planet, turning upon its axis, taking its orderly way among other planets, moving about the Sun that had usurped the "proud Centre" that for centuries had been the world of Man.

4

THE BREAKING OF THE CIRCLE

For three hundred years men have vainly tried to put together the pieces of a broken circle. Some have been poets, some philosophers, some artists. They have shared a common desire for a unity that once existed, and have sought a "return to medievalism," when life seemed integrated about a strong center, whether of the Church or of a monarch. Except for an occasional individual who has found peace in old religion, their efforts have proved fruitless. Poets and artists have deliberately revived old styles, but these attempts have been equally abortive. Modern critics have kidnapped to our times poets like Donne, in whom they find a "unified sensibility" of feeling and thinking. Philosophical poets—Pope, Wordsworth, Tennyson—have tried to express a world view, as did Lucretius for the ancients, Dante for the Middle Ages, Milton for the seventeenth-century Protestant. But all the king's horses and all the king's men cannot put Humpty-Dumpty together again. Mere fitting together of pieces may remake the picture in a jigsaw puzzle; it will not remake an egg. Nor can we reconstruct the old Circle of Perfection, broken by modern science and philosophy. Donne spoke truly when he said: "Nothing more endlesse, nothing sooner broke."

Since the seventeenth century the paths of literature

and science have divided, and the ways of one have become strange to the other. Two main issues are involved, I think: one is a matter of language, the other of basic ways of thinking about the world and man. Since the Renaissance, "style" has become a self-conscious word. Francis Bacon, in the *Advancement of Learning*, protested the "literary" language of his own period as a vehicle for science. The Royal Society, in early Restoration years, deliberately adopted a program that hastened the division between two languages, urging members—many of whom were men of letters—to put aside the "language of Wits and Scholars" and adopt a clearer, simpler style modeled upon that of "Mechanicks and Artisans." Wordsworth, protesting the poetic diction of the eighteenth century, formulated another such program. All of us are aware of various reforms recommended by our own contemporaries. In Shakespeare's day, there was little distinction between styles, often none between prose and poetry, certainly only the rudiments of any self-conscious separation between the language of the poet and that of the scientist. Kepler, as we shall see, often spoke like Dante on the one hand, Marlowe on the other. The language of poetry and of science was one when the world was one.

A more profound change has come about in attitudes toward Nature. The earlier poets did not need to develop a self-conscious "philosophy of Nature," as did Wordsworth and Tennyson. They were inextricably involved in a world and a universe that lived as they lived, in which they found exact analogies for their organic and bodily functions and for the power of their souls. Man *was* in little all the sphere. As he grew and flourished, so did his world; as he decayed and died, so too his world. God's pattern was eternally repeated in macrocosm, geocosm, microcosm. Man's head was a copy of God and the universe, not only in its shape, but in its being the seat of Reason. Man, the epitome of God and the world, was rational; so were the world and the universe, into which God had imparted some of His own rationality. Each of the three worlds had its individuality, yet each was involved with the others, and all partook of God. Only since the seventeenth century has the poet felt the necessity of bringing together what the shears of a scientific philosophy cut apart.

The pencils of our historians are clear and sharp. The new mechanistic earth appeared as the result of teachings of Copernicus, Gilbert, Galileo, Descartes, Newton, all of whom, they imply, departed radically from the old superstition of a living earth. Historians are indulgent with the poets, if they mention them at all, for poets may be allowed to lag behind the times and repeat inherited metaphor. But historians are as severe as schoolmasters with any supposed "thinker" who is caught napping and still believes in the absurd idea of a living earth after Copernicus, Kepler, Galileo have bade the sun stand still and the earth move and take its place as a mechanical part of a mechanical universe.

These historians are quite correct, of course, about *what* happened. Some of them, I think, are on less firm ground when they tell us *when* and *how* it happened. We are led to believe that the scientist cast off overnight worn garments of thinking and rose in the morning to don a complete new outfit, leaving old superstition, old religion, old belief to the poets. The change was not so abrupt as that. In my introduction to these essays, I referred to Mr. Collingwood's statement about our own thinking: "Modern cosmology, like its predecessors, is based on an analogy. What is new about it is that the analogy is a new one." I say again that one of the

most important differences between our modern attitude and
the attitude of the Platonically-minded thinkers, from the
ancients through the Renaissance, lies in our self-conscious-
ness: we know that we are making analogies. Our ancestors
believed that what we call "analogy" was *truth*, inscribed by
God in the nature of things.

My purpose in this essay is twofold: I shall try to explain
in more detail how and why the Circle of Perfection finally
broke under the impact of seventeenth-century science, and
at the same time suggest that old habits die hard, and that
time-honored ways of thinking about the world and man did
not change in a moment. The time-lag has sometimes been as
clear in scientists as in poets. I am offering no apology
for poets, who need none, though they often continue to live
in a departed world or in a world made by their own imagination. Nor do I intend a critique of science. Perhaps I am
really saying that many great scientists of the past were
poets, and some of them mystics. They made their greatest
discoveries by processes easily comprehensible to poets. They
continued to speak a language that had been common to poet
and scientist, when our forefathers still believed in a little
world that was a copy of the great world and of God.

I

Have not all soules thought
For many ages, that our body is wrought
Of Ayre and Fire, and other Elements?
And now they thinke of new ingredients,
And one Soule thinkes one, and another way
Another thinkes, and 'tis an even lay.   (*SA*, ll. 263–68)

So Donne in the *Second Anniversary*. Theories of the nature of man, like theories of the nature of the cosmos, were in confusion. Was man constituted of humors? Of elements? Were his imbalances to be corrected by the administration of "hot and dry," according to Galenic herbalists, or by chemicals, as Paracelsus declared? Paracelsus had opposed Galen; many opposed Paracelsus. So far as the layman could see, one man's guess was as good as another; it was "an even lay."

A revolution was to occur in physiology as in cosmology, and a little world of man was to die with the greater world and the universe. Human personality and character, as we have seen, had long been interpreted in terms in which the world and the universe were described. Physiology and psychology were one. Man's nature, like his body, was what the humors or the elements had made him. Later poets will not say with Shakespeare:

> His life was gentle, and the elements
> So mixed in him that Nature might stand up,
> And say to all the world, "This was a man!"

They will not pay tribute to a complete personality in such terms as Donne used of one of his "shees,"

> Shee whose Complexion was so even made,
> That which of her Ingredients should invade
> The other three, no Feare, no Art could guesse,
>
> (*SA*, ll. 123–25)

nor will they feel the close association between the humors of the body and mind and character that Donne took for granted when he wrote:

> Wee understood
> Her by her sight; her pure, and eloquent blood
> Spoke in her cheekes, and so distinctly wrought,
> That one might almost say, her body thought.
>
> (*SA*, ll. 243–46)

As man was cut off from Nature during the seventeenth century, so his mind was separated from his body. Most of all, the soul—in the medieval and Elizabethan sense—disappeared or was handed over by science to religion. It was symbolic of the new attitude that Descartes, still so close to his ancestors that he could not entirely dismiss the soul from his mechanical system as he could not entirely dismiss God, sought to localize the soul in the pineal gland. The Elizabethans were not afraid of the word *soul*. It was not something apart from the body or something that could be localized in it. It was man, the complete personality, the complex that made the individual an individual. But the time was coming when poets would no longer write, as did George Chapman in *Euthymiae Raptus*, of the happy state of the man in whom the soul had her proper empire:

> Then (like a man in health) the whole consort
> Of his tun'd body sings; which otherwise
> Is like one full of weiward maladies,
> Still out of tune.

Like his world and his universe, man had been a totality. Body, mind, and soul were one, "health" was a moral as well as a physical condition. Man was so involved in Nature that no separation was possible—nor would an Elizabethan have understood such separation. The Brights and the Burtons did not analyze melancholy purely as a state of mind; it was a state of the body, a state too of the soul. Timothy

Bright approached his problem from his training as a physician, Robert Burton from his as a clergyman, but Burton was as competent a physician on this subject as was Dr. Bright; his was, in the truest sense of the phrase, "a cure of souls." The dissociation of sensibility, which critics have found in the modern world, was impossible among men to whom thinking and feeling were parts of the same process in body, mind, and spirit. But these are matters which we may understand better after we have seen the extent to which man, like the world and universe, gradually ceased to be part of an animate universe and became mechanism, a subject for objective analysis in terms of mechanical actions and reactions.

Donne could not have anticipated all this, of course, as he could not have grasped all the implications of the "new Philosophy." Yet some of his lines may serve as a guide to confusions in physiology which his age did realize, when men were living between an old world and a new. Let us go back to that passage of his, which seems to imply that while there were almost as many schools of medicine as doctors in those schools, the learned theorists had found no cure for the most common ills of man, as they had not been able to explain the basic problem of physiology:

> Knowst thou but how the stone doth enter in
> The bladders cave, and never breake the skinne?
> Knowst thou how blood, which to the heart doth flow,
> Doth from one ventricle to th' other goe?
> And for the putrid stuffe, which thou dost spit,
> Knowst thou how thy lungs have attracted it? . . .
> What hope have wee to know our selves, when wee
> Know not the least things, which for our use be?
>
> (*SA*, ll. 269–80)

As late as 1672 Donne's first question was still being answered by an important physician in old terms of macrocosmic-microcosmic analogy, when Dr. Thomas Shirley, Physician-in-Ordinary to His Majesty Charles the Second, published an important medical treatise on "the stone," that plague of man almost as common in the seventeenth century as the "pox" and the "tertian ague." The title of Shirley's book indicates the extent to which correspondence between two worlds could still govern medical thinking: *A Philosophical Essay, declaring the probable Causes whence Stones are produced in the Greater World . . . being a Prodomus to a Medicinal Tract concerning the Causes and Cures of the Stone in the Kidneys and Bladders of Men.* Geology was proceeding in lockstep with physiology, one hampering while it thought to help the other, despite the fact that a new approach to physiology had been laid down a half-century earlier, when Harvey had answered the apparently insoluble question:

> Knowst thou how blood, which to the heart doth flow,
> Doth from one ventricle to th' other goe?

For many years Harvey himself had had no better answer to the problem than had the host of his predecessors, in spite of long years of dissection of living animals. "When I first gave my mind to vivisections, as a means of discovering the motions and uses of the heart," he wrote at the beginning of his work *Exercitatio Anatomica de Motu Cordis et Sanguinis de Animalibus,* "and sought to discover these from actual inspection, and not from the writings of others, I found the task so truly arduous, so full of difficulties, that I was almost tempted to think, with Frascastorius, that the motion of the heart was only to be comprehended by God. . . . I was not surprised that Andreas Laurentius should have written that the motion of the heart was as perplexing as the flux and re-flux of Euripus had appeared to Aristotle."

Harvey's book, in which he announced the solution of the problem of circulation in 1628, is very different from most scientific works of the earlier seventeenth century, consisting largely of careful reports of experiments with a minimum of theory, with almost no philosophizing of the kind usually found in "natural histories" of this period. There is no poetry here, and almost no overtones of any sort, even in the intro-duction in which Harvey discussed the usual belief "that the arteries carry the vital blood into the different parts, abun-dantly charged with vital spirits, which cherish the heat of these parts, sustain them when asleep, and recruit them when exhausted." "No one denies," he wrote, almost with impa-tience, "the blood as such, even the portion of it which flows in the veins, is imbued with spirits." [1] But "spirituous blood is not the less blood on that account"—and it was blood rather than spirits that interested Harvey. As he cut up an eel, tied ligatures about serpents, opened a live snake to watch the pulsa-tion of the heart, touched with his "finger wetted with sa-liva" the heart of a pigeon, studied through a magnifying glass shrimps and crayfish, to prove that they too had hearts, he was not moved to lyrical rhapsody over these little worlds made cunningly, nor did he ponder on the divine repetition of larger worlds in lesser. His discovery "that there is a kind of rhythm" preserved between the "two motions, one of the ventricles, the other of the auricles" might have led that later physician, Sir Thomas Browne, to a charming disquisition on the music of the spheres, the cosmic dance, or the pre-established harmony of God. But Harvey—in more than

[1] William Harvey, *Of the Motion of the Heart and Blood in Animals*, trans. by Robert Willis, rev. by Alexander Bowie (London, 1889), Introduc-tion.

chronology—was the contemporary of Galileo, the predecessor of Descartes and Newton, with their world-machines. His mind turned not to animism but to mechanism:

Nor is this [harmony] for any other reason than it [the heart] is a piece of machinery, in which, though one wheel gives motion to another, yet all the wheels seem to move simultaneously; or in that mechanical contrivance which is adapted to firearms, where, the trigger being touched, down comes the flint, strikes against the steel, elicits a spark, which falling among the powder, ingites it, when the flame extends, enters the barrel, causes the explosion, propels the ball, and the mark is attained.[2]

Exact in his observations, empirical in his method, literal in his style, Harvey seems as far removed from the poetical and mystical tendencies of his age as any modern scientist could ask. Yet even he could not completely dissociate himself from ways of thinking ingrained in man for centuries. The analogy between macrocosm and microcosm still lingered in his mind; so too the Circle of Perfection. Indeed Harvey's capitalization in his startling announcement indicates the importance of the circle as the clue to the circulation of the blood. Originally he had taken for granted, like earlier physiologists, that the blood in the veins and the blood in the arteries were two separate streams; but the more he experimented, the more incapable he found himself of reaching a satisfactory explanation of the phenomena "unless the blood should somehow find its way from the arteries into the veins, and so return to the right side of the heart." "I began," he says, "to think whether there might not be a MOTION, AS IT WERE, IN A CIRCLE. Now, this I afterwards found to be true." Inevitably he went back to the macrocosm and microcosm: The motion of the blood is circular

[2] *Ibid.*, chapter V.

in the same way as Aristotle says that the air and the rain emulate the circular motion of the superior bodies; for the moist earth, warmed by the sun, evaporates; the vapours drawn upwards are condensed, and descending in the form of rain, moisten the earth again. By this arrangement are generations of living things produced; and in like manner are tempests and meteors engendered by the circular motion, and by the approach and recession of the sun.[3]

As in the great world, so in the small: through the motion of the blood, all parts of the body "are nourished, cherished, quickened by the warmer, more perfect, vapours, spirituous, and, as I may say, alimentive blood," which, having made its circular journey "returns to its sovereign, the heart, as if to its source, or to the inmost home of the body, there to recover its state of excellence and of perfection."

Harvey had discovered the process of circulation in terms of the mechanism of the heart; but he had not solved the greater mystery of the heart. He needed no "ethereal spirits" in order to chart the course of the circulation, yet he sought the aid of such spirits in order to explain the passage of heat from the sun, who warmed and nourished the world, to the heart, source of blood that warmed and nourished the animal. Only in the sections in which he discusses such mysteries does Harvey resort to what scientists would consider rhetoric. As the sun to the universe, so the heart to the little world:

The heart . . . is the beginning of life; the sun of the microcosm, even as the sun in his turn might well be designated the heart of the world. . . . It is the household divinity which, discharging its function, nourishes, cherishes, quickens the whole body, and is indeed the foundation of life. . . . Since death is a corruption which takes place through deficiency of heat, and since all living things

[3] *Ibid.*, chapter VIII.

are warm, all dying things cold, there must be a particular seat and fountain, a kind of home and hearth, where the cherisher of nature, the original of the native fire, is stored and preserved; from which heat and life are dispensed to all parts as from a fountain head. . . . Now, that the heart is this place, that the heart is the principle of life, . . . I trust no one will deny.[4]

There is little other rhetoric in the bare, clear unadorned style of Harvey's volume; and—except on these few occasions—little universal analogy. In so far as man could break with the past, Harvey put aside older ways of thinking, as older ways of writing. The body of man was not to him "the Marvels of Marvels," the "Mundum Magnum, a world to which all the rest of the world is subordinate." The body of man, like the bodies of eels, serpents, crayfish, was a "subject" for dissection, exposed upon a laboratory table before a scientist who objectively studied its processes and found in the little world a series of machines, operating upon mechanical principles.

Harvey was speaking a new language to ears still attuned to the old. The early reception of his theory was far from spectacular. As he himself said, "Some chid and calumniated me, and laid it to me as a crime that I had dared to depart from the precepts and opinions of all anatomists." Others, more willing to listen, did not at first believe that he had proved his case. His ideas met with skepticism on the Continent, and for a time evoked little general enthusiasm in the more receptive England. After his death in the mid-century, all that was changed, and Restoration England (as capable of thinking in terms of mechanical hearts as of mechanical universes), claimed him as "her boast and pride." One of Cowley's stanzas in his *Ode upon Dr. Harvey* shows amus-

[4] *Ibid.*

ingly how Harvey's "Circle" remained an object of praise, when the circles of poets were dismissed as symbols of conservatism and convention:

> Methinks in Arts great Circle others stand
> Lock'd up together, hand in hand,
> Ev'ry one leads as he is led,
> The same bare path they tread,
> A Dance like Fairies, a Fantastick round;
> But neither change their motion, nor their ground;
> Had Harvey to this Road confin'd his Wit,
> His noble Circle of the Blood, had been untrodden yet.

Whatever the attitude of physiologists, popular interest in Harvey's theories was less the result of the fact that he had explained the problem of the circulation of the blood in animals than that he seemed to have solved the greater mystery of the circulation of the waters of the earth in streams, rivers, seas. Here we find a good example of the extent to which analogies from one science, read into another, succeeded in retarding the progress of the second. The poets will help us understand a geological dilemma that had interested scientists and philosophers for centuries. In one stanza of *The Purple Island* Fletcher repeated a commonplace long accepted in both physiology and geology about the body of man and the body of the earth:

> Nor is there any part in all this land,
> But is a little Isle; for thousand brooks
> In azure chanels glide on silver sand;
> Their serpent windings, and deceiving crooks
> Circling about, and wat'ring all the plain,
> Emptie themselves into th' all drinking main;
> And creeping forward slide, but never turn again. (II.9)

Raleigh had written in his *History of the World:* "His blood, which disperseth itself by the branches of veins through all the body, may be resembled to those waters which are carried by brooks and rivers over all the earth." Davies said in *Orchestra:*

> Yet though the Earth is ever steadfast seene,
> On her broad breast hath Dauncing ever beene.
> For those blew vaines that through her body spred,
> Those saphire streames which from great hills do spring,
> (The Earths great duggs; for every wight is fed
> With sweet fresh moisture from them issuing):
> Observe a daunce in their wilde wandering. (Stanzas 51–52)

Centuries before Fletcher and Raleigh and Davies the similarity between blood in the veins and arteries in man's body and water in the rivers and streams of earth had been a commonplace, as can be seen from *The Mirror of the World,*[5] a medieval encyclopedia so important that Caxton reprinted it:

All in like wise as the blood of a man goeth and renneth by the veins of the body and goeth out and issueth in some place, all in like wise renneth the water by the veins of the earth and sourdeth and springeth out by the fountains and wells.

Few problems of the earth had been debated longer than the question of the origin of springs and rivers. Anaxagoras and Plato had taught that from a vast cavern within the earth, filled with waters in constant motion, all rivers flowed and from it all proceeded. Since both philosophers were fortunately vague about the processes of issue and return, there seemed no conflict between their theories and the few Biblical suggestions of the origin of waters. Moses' statement about

[5] Quoted by E. M. W. Tillyard, *Elizabethan World Picture* (New York, 1944), p. 85.

the Flood was specific only in its chronology: "In the sixth hundredth year of Noah's life, in the second month, the seventeenth day of the month, the same day were all the fountains of the great deep broken up." Equally vague were the frequently-quoted words of Ecclesiastes: "All the rivers run into the sea; yet the sea is not full; unto the place from whence the rivers come, thither shall they return again." The Fathers had spent much ink upon the problem of the origin of springs and rivers. Did they arise from the sea? How then did they flow back to land? Were they a part of those waters God commanded to be gathered together when the dry land appeared? But if the original waters were salt, how explain the fact that the rivers and streams were fresh? And if the original waters were fresh, how came the salt in the sea? For centuries ingenuity had crowded upon subtlety, producing answers to those riddles that sound to our ears as curious as the profundities of the Walrus,

> And why the sea is boiling hot?
> And whether pigs have wings?

In spite of Aristotle, the rivers of Plato, of Moses, of Ecclesiastes had continued to confuse the issue for centuries by mingling their fresh waters with salt, so that the orthodox found it necessary to sweeten their waters by logical theories.

As confusing as the various kinds of waters on the earth had seemed, even to Harvey, the various kinds of blood in the body of man, one in the arteries, the other in the veins. Phineas Fletcher's gloss on the quoted stanza will tell us the difference:

The whole body is as it were watered with great plenty of rivers, veins, arteries, and nerves. A vein is a vessel long, round, hollow, rising from the liver, appointed to contein, concoct and distribute the bloud; . . . the colour of this bloud is purple. An arterie is a vessel long, round, hollow, formed for conveyance of that more spritely bloud, which is elaborate in the heart. This bloud is frothy, yellowish, full of spirits.   (*The Purple Island*, II.9)

The veins, declared Fletcher, "convey nourishment from the liver . . . from the liver rise all the springs of bloud, which runnes in the veins." The arteries, on the other hand, "convey life and heat from the heart." The liver was still to Fletcher, as it had been for two thousand years, the most important organ of the body, "the Isle's great Steward," from whence all is dispersed. Indeed Fletcher was more classical and medieval than many of his contemporaries, since he still held that the liver, rather than the heart, was the seat of love.

Harvey's work, proving that the blood in the veins is the same blood as in the arteries, and that its circulation is controlled by the heart, had been published for five years when *The Purple Island* appeared, yet Fletcher showed no awareness that the old theories of arterial and venous blood had been disproved.[6] Later poets, however, seized upon a new source for figures of speech, though their interest was usually rather in the origin of rivers and streams than in the circulation of the blood itself. Henry Vaughan, physician and lover of nature, reinterpreted his favorite river Usk in physiological terms:

[6] A. B. Langdale in *Phineas Fletcher, Man of Letters, Science, and Divinity* (New York, 1937), pp. 192 ff., insists that the last line of Fletcher's stanza, quoted above, shows his knowledge of Harvey. Fletcher's gloss, however, proves that Fletcher still followed the most conventional belief that the blood in the arteries differed from that in the veins, and that the liver was the important organ, so far as blood was concerned. The originality of Harvey's discovery was less in the theory *that blood circulates*, which others had suggested, than in demonstration of the process by which circulation is effected.

So where swift Isca from our lofty hills
With lowd farewells descends, and foming fills
A wider Channel, like som great port-vein . . .

Perhaps Crashaw was not thinking of geology and physiology when he wrote in *Sospetto d'Herode:*

Below the Botome of the great Abysse,
There where one Center reconciles all things,
The world's profound Heart pants,

but Thomas Traherne, who followed new science closely, intended a double meaning in *The Circulation* when he wrote

All Things to Circulations owe
Themselvs; by which alone
They do exist,

and went on to find circulation everywhere—in the "thirsty earth," the springs, the "seas that pour out their streams In springs, those streams repair," the earth that "no exhalations would afford, / Were not its spirits by the Sun restored," reaching his climax in God and the soul:

He is the Primitive Eternal Spring
The Endless Ocean of each Glorious Thing.
          The Soul a Vessel is
     A Spacious Bosom to Contain
     All the fair Treasures of his Bliss,
Which run like Rivers from, into the Main,
And all it doth receiv returns again.

In the early years of the century Fulke Greville had used the older conception of the waters of the earth for a figure of speech to describe *Learning:*

     Learning, like a Caspian Sea,
Hath hitherto receiv'd all little brookes,

> Devour'd all their sweetnesse, borne their names away,
> And in her greennesse hid their chrystall lookes;
> Let her turn Ocean now, and give back more,
> To those cleare Springs, than she receiv'd before.

Post-Harveian Denham, however, in *The Progress of Learning*, following old geology but new physiology, showed that it was as possible to freshen metaphors as to sweeten salt water:

> Our God, when Heaven and earth He did create,
> Form'd Man, who should of both participate;
> If our lives motions theirs must imitate,
> Our knowledge, like our blood, should circulate.
>
> Into earth's spungy veins the ocean sinks,
> These rivers, to replenish which he drinks;
> So learning, which from reason's fountain springs,
> Back to the source some secret channel brings.

Philosophers like Henry More found in Harvey's theory an explanation for geological processes they did not yet understand. "The Sea is the Fountain of Moisture," wrote More, "and administers to the Springs underneath, as the Springs supply the Rivers above-ground, and so imitate the Circulation of the Blood in Man's Body."

Not until 1673 when Pierre Perrault, a French amateur of science, measured the rainfall and drainage in the Seine basin, and proved what Leonardo da Vinci and Bernard Palissy had surmised—that rain and snow are the causes of rivers and springs—did this particular belief in correspondence begin to fade, and the waters of the earth take their way without assistance of Harvey's theory. Only gradually did science put an end to the old myth and leave to poets the heart of the deep from which all rivers proceeded and back to which they took their circular way. Old habits die hard. For one Harvey, who so far as possible in his time replaced the older animate nature by a series of mechanical operations, there were a dozen who still thought in terms of microcosmic-macrocosmic analogy.

II

In his own day William Gilbert of Colchester enjoyed more fame than did William Harvey in his. They were to go down to posterity together, praised by their countrymen as the two greatest British pre-Newtonian scientists. Proud of its part in exploration and discovery, England was equally proud that the great developments in the magnetic needle and in the study of magnetism were English. Dryden wrote in his *Epistle to Dr. Walter Charleton*,

> Gilbert shall live till loadstones cease to draw,
> Or British fleets the boundless ocean awe.

"Whoever gave the first Hint of this Invention," wrote John Wallis in a paper read before the Royal Society and published in the *Philosophical Transactions* in 1701–2, "certain it is, that the great Improvements of the Magnetick Doctrine are due to the English. . . . And Mr. Gilbert's Notion (of the Earths whole Body being but one great Magnet; and lesser Magnets being so many Terrella's sympathizing with the whole) is English too."

Gilbert believed that his revolt from the styles in which earlier science had been written was as complete as his revolt from authority. In 1600 he dedicated the *De Magnete*, "these foundations of magnetic science," "a new style of philosophizing" to the "true philosophers, ingenuous minds" who looked for knowledge in things themselves rather than in the books of the ancients, and called the attention of his readers to the style he had adopted: he had not "brought into this work any graces of rhetoric, any verbal ornateness," but had used only "such terms as are needed to make what is said clearly intelligible." [7] In a work so self-consciously designed as a break with the past, we might expect to find ourselves on unfamiliar territory, to learn a "new science" in new language strange to our ears. But we shall be more at home with Gilbert than with Harvey. One must seek carefully through Harvey's work to discover those few passages in which he still thought in terms of macrocosm and microcosm. Such analogy was constantly in Gilbert's mind; indeed, he will add still another sphere to our circles, and show us a more minute little world than we have found, a little world containing within itself all the properties of the great earth. Sir Kenelm Digby in his *Treatise of Bodies* said very truly: "This great man arrived to discover so much of magnetical philosophy . . . by forming a little load-stone into the shape of the earth. But which means he compassed a wonderful designe, which was to make the whole globe of the earth maniable; for he found the properties of the whole earth, in that little body; which he therefore called a *terrella*, or little earth."

As Harvey had spent his days studying the hearts of animals, Gilbert had spent his studying loadstones. He described in detail many of them, of all sizes and shapes and varying powers. From them all, he chose for his demonstration of the nature of the magnetic earth a loadstone fashioned in the shape of a globe, "inasmuch as the spherical form, which too is the most perfect, agrees best with the earth, which is a

[7] William Gilbert of Colchester, *On the Loadstone and Magnetic Bodies*, trans. by P. F. Mottelay (London, 1893), Author's Preface.

globe." Upon this stone he philosophized, as Harvey seldom did upon his hearts. For a moment we feel ourselves
back in the world of the poets:

The stone thus prepared is a true homogeneous offspring of the
earth and is of the same shape, having got from art the orbicular
form that nature in the beginning gave to earth, the common
mother; and it is a natural little body, endowed with a multitude
of properties, whereby many abstruse and unheeded truths of philosophy may be more readily brought to the knowledge of mankind.[8]

To his rounded stone he gave the name "Μίκρογη (Microge)
or *Terrella* (earthkin, little earth)." On the *terrella,* as upon
earth, he distinguished "mathematical circles"; the loadstone
had its "natural equator," its Tropic of Capricorn; it had, too,
poles which were not artificial "mathematical points, but natural points of force." It had the power of direction and of
standing still at north and south; it had also "a circular motion
to the earth's position, whereby it adjusts itself to the earth's
law." As man was in little all the sphere, to Gilbert the
loadstone was in little all the earth:

The loadstone and all magnetic bodies . . . seem to contain
within themselves the potency of the earth's core and of its inmost
viscera, and to have and comprise whatever in the earth's substance is privy and inward; the loadstone possesses the actions peculiar to the globe, of attraction, polarity, revolution, of taking
positions in the universe according to the law of the whole; it contains the supreme excellences of the globe and orders them: all
this in token and proof a certain eminent combination and of a
most accordant nature. . . . The loadstone far surpasses all other
bodies around us in the virtues and properties that pertain to the
common mother of us all.[9]

[8] *Ibid.,* I.iii.23.   [9] *Ibid.,* I.xvii.66.

As man was a little copy of God and the universe, so Gilbert's loadstone was an epitome of the great earth. And by the kind of reasoning with which we have become familiar, Gilbert, having discovered the principle of the small world, read that principle back into the earth as he announced his epoch-making discovery: "That the Terrestrial Globe is Magnetic and is a Load-Stone; and just as in our Hands the Loadstone possesses all the Primary Powers of the Earth, so the Earth by reason of the same Potencies lies ever in the same Direction with the Universe." Here again is the repetition of worlds, the greater formed upon analogy with the small world of the *terrella* Gilbert held in his hand. Here is the circle; here too the old emphasis upon center and circumference, even though Gilbert's interpretation of both center and circumference is quite different from anything man had thought before: "The centre of this sphere is not in the pole (as Baptista Porta declares), but in the centre of the stone and the terrella. So, too, the earth's centre is the centre of the earth's magnetic movements. . . . The rays of magnetic force are dispersed in a circle in all directions; . . . Thus the centre and middle of the terrella is the centre of force, and thence to the circumference of its sphere of influence its magnetic virtues extend for equal distances in all directions." So too the "Orbis Virtutis" of the earth.

Had Gilbert lived a generation later, he would undoubtedly have interpreted the power of his loadstone and of his magnetic earth in terms of mechanism. But Gilbert was an Elizabethan. His earth was still the animate earth he had inherited from Thales through a long train of philosophers and scientists. He was Elizabethan, too, in that it seemed to him entirely natural that the earth should have its "soul." That soul he also read over from earth again into his *terrella*. "The Magnetic Force," he began one of his most important chapters, "is Animate, or Imitates a Soul; in many Respects it Surpasses the Human Soul while that is United to an Organic Body." Gilbert had cast aside the adornments of rhetoric, but he could not write of the soul of his little earth without emotion:

Wonderful is the loadstone shown in many experiments to be, and, as it were, animate. And this one eminent property is the same which the ancients held to be a soul in the heavens, in the globes, and in the stars, in sun and moon. . . . And I wonder much why the globe of earth with its effluences should have been by Aristotle and his followers condemned and driven into exile and cast out of all the fair order of the glorious universe, as being brute and soulless. . . . As for us, we deem the whole world animate, and all globes, all stars, and this glorious earth, too, we hold to be from the beginning by their own desinate souls governed and from them also to have the impulse of self-preservation. . . . Pitiable is the state of the stars, abject the lot of earth, if this high dignity of soul is denied them, while it is granted to the worm, the ant, the roach, to plants and morels. . . . Wherefore not without reason, Thales . . . declares the loadstone to be animate, a part of the animate mother earth and her beloved offspring.[10]

Gilbert was writing science, and his place in the history of science is secure. Yet he still thought as poets thought, and in spite of himself he often wrote as poets wrote of a living world and a living universe, and of the mysterious power God had implanted in their souls, which he found repeated even in the tiny *terrella* "sympathizing with the whole," that "natural little body endowed with a multitude of properties whereby many abstruse and unheeded truths of philosophy, hid in deplorable darkness, may be more readily brought to the knowledge of mankind."

Gilbert did not live to prove the importance in the cosmic

[10] *Ibid.*, v.xii.308–12.

scheme of that force and power he found in the loadstone
and in the earth, emanating from a center to a circumference
which was everywhere. He was too close to the beginnings
of the "new Philosophy" to understand the full import of his
own teaching. Kepler, Galileo, Descartes were still to come
before Newton formulated the law of the universe. Gilbert,
of course, knew only Copernicus, whose theories he did not
accept *in toto*, though he devoted the last long section of the
De Magnete to insistence upon the truth of one aspect of
Copernicanism—the diurnal rotation of the earth.

III

Gilbert's conclusion leads us back again to the problem
of the "new Philosophy" that called all in doubt to Donne
eleven years after Gilbert had published his work. Let us
pause over some of Donne's details before going on to discover the basic presuppositions of another important scientist
who was largely responsible for the breaking of the cosmic
circles in which Donne had found evidence for beauty, symmetry, and proportion:

> And new Philosophy calls all in doubt,
> The Element of fire is quite put out;
> The Sun is lost, and th' earth, and no mans wit
> Can well direct him where to looke for it.   (*FA*, ll. 205–8)

That "the Sun is lost, and th' earth" is clear enough: Copernicus had changed the places of both, and man looked at the
heavens with unfamiliar eyes. If the planets still moved in
circles, they moved about another center, including in their
cosmic dance the earth which had become merely a planet.
But what of the line immediately preceding? In the *Second*

Anniversary Donne returned to this problem when he said, in his description of the progress of the soul to heaven,

> she stayes not in the ayre,
> To looke what Meteors there themselves prepare;
> She carries no desire to know, nor sense,
> Whether th' ayres middle region be intense;
> For th' Element of fire, she doth not know,
> Whether she past by such a place or no.   (*SA*, ll. 189–94)

But in 1611 Donne had found additional reason for despondency when he realized that "the element of fire is quite put out." Tycho and others had declared that there was no such circle of fire between the earth and the moon as Aristotle had presupposed and men generally had believed, but it was less Tycho than his younger assistant Kepler who brought that truth home to such men as Donne, by a simple optical demonstration that "if there were a sphere of fire under the moon, considerable refraction of the rays emitted from the stars should be evident." [11] The orb of fire was destroyed, as were those other solid orbs in which man had long believed. Still another circle had broken. But what of the great circles of the planets? Did they not remain, even though the solid orbs were gone, even though the center of the planets was now the sun?

> We thinke the heavens enjoy their Sphericall,
> Their round proportion embracing all.
> But yet their various and perplexed course,
> Observ'd in divers ages, doth enforce
> Men to finde out so many Eccentrique parts,
> Such divers downe-right lines, such overthwarts,
> As disproportion that pure forme. . . .
>   nor can the Sunne

[11] See Charles Monroe Coffin, *John Donne and the New Philosophy* (New York, 1938), p. 169.

> Perfit a Circle, or maintaine his way
> One inch direct; but where he rose to-day
> He comes no more, but with a couzening line,
> Steales by that point, and so is Serpentine. . . .
> So of the Starres which boast that they doe runne
> In Circle still, none ends where he begun.   (*FA*, ll. 251–76)

This is not all "new Philosophy"; indeed many of Donne's lines deal with astronomical ideas known to the ancients; while others refer to Ptolemaic conceptions. The new astronomy had served only to sharpen problems and discrepancies already implicit in the old. Old and new together, however, they "disproportioned that pure forme" which laymen had believed existed in the heavens. Charles Monroe Coffin has analyzed all these lines in detail, and I shall pause over only one idea, which he does not stress, but which I believe lay behind Donne's feeling that the "Sphericall" and "round proportion" once enjoyed by the heavens could no longer be proved. In 1609 Kepler had published *De Motibus Stellae Martis*, his commentary on the planet Mars, in which he set down the first two of what we now call "Kepler's laws," demonstrating the fact that the planets move about the sun not in circles but in ellipses, formulating the law governing their motion. The existence of the most perfect circles of all had been disproved, ironically enough by a scientist who had felt the beauty and the mystery of the circle more profoundly than had Donne and professed poets.

Modern historians of science usually approach Kepler with some misgiving, unless they belong to the group that reads its early science only in extracts carefully selected by anthologists for their scientific value. Newton disturbs the others somewhat: he should not have been more concerned over his apocalyptical interpretations than he was about the law of gravity; he should not have been influenced by such a mystic as Jacob Boehme—yet he was. But Kepler bewilders them even more. They cannot deny the importance of his laws, but they deplore his superstition and his mysticism. The *furor poeticus* may be all very well in a poet, but a scientist should not have interlarded his serious work with poetry, nor intoxicated himself with words, as did Kepler. Kepler believed that the earth was alive and that its nature corresponded to the nature of a living universe; he believed in the sacred mystery of numbers, particularly the numbers THREE, FIVE, SEVEN; he believed in God. His way of thinking did not seem strange to Sir Thomas Browne, who wrote his most famous work to prove that a scientist may be deeply religious and felt with Kepler that an undevout astronomer must be mad. If Kepler was obsessed, it was not with superstition but with religion, religion of a sort that has long disappeared from modern science.

If we were not familiar with both the ideas and the language, we might well share the bewilderment of modern scientists when we read such a passage as this:

As the body produces hair on the skin, so the earth produces plants and trees, and as in the former lice are generated, so in the latter caterpillars, crickets, and many other insects and sea-monsters. As the body exudes moisture in tears and sweat through the pores, so does the earth exude amber and bitumen. As urine from the bladder, rivers flow from the mountains. As the body discharges winds that reek of sulphur and are inflammable, so the earth has its sulphur in subterranean fires, in thunder and lightning. As in the veins of living beings are formed blood and sweat, exuded through the passages of the body, so in the veins of the earth are metals and petrifactions, and from them issue steamy torrents. As other living beings take into their bodies food and drink, the earth,

through its channels, draws into itself stuff of which much is con-
cocted. It swallows the waters of the sea so that the ocean, in spite
of the constant flowing of rivers, never overflows.[12]

This is not Paracelsus Bombast; it is a section of Kepler's
"The Earth as a Living Being" in the *Harmonice Mundi*, a
section, indeed, leading to one of his statements on the "dy-
namic power" of matter, which he called "energy." We read
in the histories that "Kepler replaced the notion of soul, the
animism of the earlier thinkers, by the notion of physical
energy." Such was his effect, yet his passages on energy are
usually embedded, as here, in others developing his belief
that the world possesses both a living body with senses and a
soul with memory, which, as he says here, like a pregnant
woman, has the potency of producing from itself something
apart from itself. The soul of the earth is a flame "in which
the image of the Divine Countenance is imprinted." The
earth-soul reflects the cosmic soul: "For the Creator has in
himself not only the geometrical archetypes of all things that
He has made, but also the divine plan for all the phenomena
still to be created. Hence the earth-soul reflects in itself the
image of the zodiac and of the firmament, evidence of the in-
terrelation and the homogeneity of terrestrial and celestial
things." In the energy of the earth is the essence of the soul:
"It is the steady burning of a flame." God himself is the "essence of energy," and, as the "essence of the flame is in its
burning, so the essence of the image of God lies in its activity,
its energy."

His conception of God is central to everything Kepler ever
wrote. It was religion rather than science that first attracted

[12] My quotations from Kepler (with the exceptions noted) are based upon
a translation made by my former colleague, Professor Anita Ascher of Smith
College.

the young Kepler to Copernicanism. As E. A. Burtt has pointed out, both Copernicus and Kepler were sun-worshipers. I borrow from Professor Burtt a passage he has translated from the *De Revolutionibus* of Copernicus:

Then in the middle of the all stands the sun. For who, in our most beautiful temple, could set this light in another or better place, than that from which it can at once illuminate the whole? Not to speak of the fact that not unfittingly do some call it the light of the world, others the soul, still others the governor. Tremegistus calls it the visible God; Sophocles' Electra, the All-seer. And in fact does the sun, seated on his royal throne, guide his family of planets as they circle round him.[13]

In one of his youthful works, Kepler went farther than Copernicus:

Of all the bodies in the universe the most excellent is the sun, whose whole essence is nothing else than the purest light, than which there is no greater star; which singly and alone is the producer, conserver, and warmer of all things; it is a fountain of light, rich in fruitful heat, most fair, limpid and pure to the sight . . . called king of the planets for his motion, heart of the world for his power, its eye for his beauty, and which alone we should judge worthy of the Most High God, should he be pleased with a material domicile, and choose a place in which to dwell with the blessed angels.[14]

From such sun-worship Kepler never recovered. Throughout his works the Sun is equated with the Father. Lover of the mystic THREE, he persistently read the Trinity into the phenomena of the heavens, as when he wrote in the *Harmonice Mundi:* "The number THREE is represented in the sphere by the surface, the centre, the content; in the station-

---

[13] Edwin A. Burtt, *Metaphysical Foundations of Physics* (New York, 1932), p. 45.
[14] *Ibid.,* p. 48.

ary world by the fixed stars, the sun and the ether; in the divine Trinity by the Father, the Son and the Holy Ghost. As the Sun dwells in the midst of the planets, at rest, yet the source of motion, he is the image of God the Father, the Creator. The relation of God to his creation is that of the Sun to motion; and as the Father is the Creator in the Trinity, so the Sun is the source of motion among the stars."

Commenting upon the Nineteenth Psalm, which deals with Creation, Kepler said: "Clearly the Psalmist was not pretending to speak as an astronomer, for otherwise he would not have failed to mention the five planets, since there is no more admirable, more beautiful, more suitable evidence to thinking men of the wisdom of the Creator than their motions." He described his "rapture" when he realized that Plato's five regular solids afforded a clue to the distance between the orbits of the planets. Yet much as he loved those five regular solids, which play so large a part in his system, he loved the circle more. "Nothing has been created by God without design," he wrote in the *Harmonice Mundi*. "Among geometrical bodies, six have been distinguished with special significance: the sphere, and the five regular solids. The spherical is part of the outermost heaven, for the world is twofold, both moving and at rest. The latter is an image of the Divine Being, considered in itself, the former an image of God the Creator. The curved line is to be compared with God, the straight with his creatures." "Why did God, in adorning the universe," he asked in the *Mysterium Cosmographicum*,

consider and heed the difference between the straight and the curved, and [prefer] the nobleness of the curved? Because the most perfect Architect must of necessity create a work of the greatest beauty. Since the Creator conceived in his mind the idea of the universe, and since that idea contained what is existent and perfect, in order that the work created might likewise be perfect . . . he could not have taken the idea for the pattern of the universe from anything but his own Being. . . . This image of himself, this idea, God imprinted upon the universe, that this might be the best and most beautiful world. . . . So the wisest of Creators created dimensions and devised quantities, the nature of which coincides with the difference between the straight and the curved. . . . And the curved represents to us God.

Like the world and the universe, the soul of the world and the universe is a circle; and the soul of man, too, is at least potentially circular. Kepler takes us back to that circle whose circumference is nowhere, whose center is everywhere. Since the soul possesses energy, it moves from its seat, the center, to the circle. When it reaches out to "feel" external objects, these "acts of sensation are grouped about it circularly." "Every soul carries the circle in itself, not only abstracted from matter, but also in a way from dimension, so that centre and circle fall together, and the soul is an extended circle, as well as a centre without circumference."

Lover of the circle as of the sun, Kepler long took for granted that the planets must inevitably move in that perfect form. Indeed he was retarded in his study of planetary motion by this presupposition. When gradually the mathematician was forced to the conclusion that the planets moved in ellipses, the mystic was bewildered. One who reads his passages sympathetically against the background of their time will appreciate his dilemma and better understand the work in which he announced his first two laws. I hope I do not misrepresent his feeling when I paraphrase him thus: circular motion still remains the perfect motion, and the circle is always a symbol of God. If the planets do not move in circles, the limitation is not in the Creator but in the creature;

the planets sought the circle, but in so far as they are not only spirit but matter, possessing limitations of grossness not shared by the Creator who is pure spirit, they move not in perfect circles but in ellipses, "imitating" so far as their natures permit "the beauty and the nobleness of the curved." Reluctantly and against his own desire Kepler broke the perfect Circle in the heavens.

Kepler's place as mathematician is secure. If his approach to mathematics was by way of a God who always geometrizes, his conclusions have stood the test of time. As metaphysician he seems on very shaky ground, so far as modern philosophers are concerned. He was a mystic, not a philosopher: mystically he found a way to truth even though the truth which modern science accepts in his work is only a small part of the whole. Kepler's "new Philosophy" was not that of a logician or metaphysician. Like the poets his was an aesthetic response, a gratification in a beautiful and glorious universe erected by the Great Geometer in which Kepler found the "mystical Mathematicks of the City of Heaven."

> Nature and Nature's laws lay hid in night.
> God said, "Let Newton be!" and all was Light.

Pope wrote the perfect epitaph for the Newton who was the father of modern science, the Newton who in his *Principia* formulated the fundamental law of the universe and described that universe as it continued to be described until yesterday. The Newton who gave the final death-blow to the old theory of an animate earth, who proved that both the world and the earth are mechanism, was the direct descendant of Galileo and Descartes. But there was another Newton, more concerned with his interpretations of Daniel [15] than with the

---

[15] The great importance of apocalyptical interpretation in this period is abundantly proved by Ernest Lee Tuveson, *Millennium and Utopia* (Berkeley and Los Angeles, 1949).

mechanical laws of the universe, a Newton who was the son of Kepler, the mystic. It was the other Newton who added the last mysterious passages to the *Principia,* and who in both *Principia* and *Opticks* presupposed a "cosmic spirit" pervading all things, exciting sensation and volition in men and animals who were less mechanical than animate. I have often wondered whether that Newton felt that his formulation of the law of gravitation was not so much the beginning of something new as the climax of something very old. Here was the ultimate proof that the microcosm does reflect the macrocosm, that there is a repetition, interrelationship, interlocking between parts and whole, long surmised by classical, medieval, Renaissance scientists, poets, mystics: the law that governs the planets and restrains the stars in their macrocosmic courses is the same law that controls the falling of a weight from the Tower of Pisa or the feather from the wing of a bird in the little world, of which man still remains the center.

IV

In this chapter and in Chapter 3 I have tried to suggest some of the complex causes that brought about the breaking of Donne's Circle of Perfection when the "new Philosophy" seemed to call all in doubt. New Philosophy, as we have seen, was far from being the only cause of pessimism in 1611. The discoveries of Galileo, with implications that were read into them, served merely to bring to a climax attitudes which had been persistent for many years, as the death of Elizabeth had sharpened awareness that the old order was changing—for the worse, conservatives believed—in the little world of England.

Donne turned not to new but to old philosophy when

he asked: "But keeps the earth her round proportion still?" and answered his own question in the negative. The perfect sphere of the earth was distorted and ugly through the sin of man. So far as astronomy was concerned, here too the new served to dramatize to laymen confusions and inconsistencies which astronomers had already found in the old. Galileo's telescopic observations proved what Copernicus, and Greek philosophers long before him had surmised, that the sun was lost and the earth, and no man's wit could well direct him where to look for it. The discovery not only of two *novae* but of unseen stars in profusion was merely a climax to ideas of decay and disintegration that had been persistent in classical, Jewish, and Christian thinking. The suggestion that some of these changes indicated decay in sun or moon was only another prophecy of the end of the world, long anticipated by religious teachers. One circle had broken in the commonwealth of England; another in the irregularity of earth's surface; the greatest of all in the movements of the heavenly bodies. All was in pieces, all coherence gone for Donne, in whose life these changes in the external world and universe coincided with a period of unusual personal difficulty. After all, as Theodore Spencer pointed out, Donne and Hamlet were men of about the same age, experiencing the same world-sorrow at crucial moments in their own careers.

But John Donne did not live to see the final crashing down of the *flammantia moenia mundi,* the utter disruption of the Circle of Perfection. He went only so far as to say:

> And freely men confesse that this world's spent,
> When in the Planets, and the Firmament
> They seeke so many new.   (*FA*, ll. 209–11)

In my *Voyages to the Moon* I have traced that theme in detail, trying to show how old literary and philosophical ideas

of other worlds than this came back with new meaning after
Galileo's proof that the moon was a world like our world,
with mountains and valleys, perhaps with water. Though
Galileo later denied that last possibility, other important
thinkers accepted it, and human imagination was stirred by
the possibility that somehow, some time, man might travel to
the moon, to find other living beings like or unlike himself.
In the *Second Anniversary* Donne's voyaging soul on its way
to heaven paid no more attention to the new world in the
moon than to the circle of fire:

> She baits not at the Moone, nor cares to trie
> Whether in that new world, men live, and die,
>
> (Lines 195–96)

But Milton's Satan and Milton's Angel considered the possibility of a world in the moon,

> if land be there,
> Fields and inhabitants? Her spots thou seest
> As clouds, and clouds may rain, and rain produce
> Fruits in her softened soil for some to eat,
> Allotted there.   (*PL*, VIII.144–48)

Others went further than Milton, and the idea of a world in
the moon became a theme for romance and satire, but a theme,
too, with immensely serious implications for man who had
once been the sole son of God. If not in the moon, then perhaps in the planets, life might exist, and if not in our cosmic
universe, then beyond in the myriads of cosmic universes
created by a "new Philosophy," which was an old philosophy.

Copernicus and his immediate followers sowed a wind;
the next generation reaped a whirlwind. The complete shat-
tering of the circle was the result of an old idea that came

back with new meaning and apparent proof: *the idea of the infinity of the universe and an infinity of worlds.* That conception had little to do with the Copernican hypothesis as we understand the phrase, though it was implied in the Copernican system. To what extent it was precipitated in England by Giordano Bruno, time may tell, for the problem of the influence of Bruno in seventeenth-century England is a teasing one, yet unsolved. But whether the ideas of infinity, so widely discussed, rejected, accepted, came from Bruno or Copernicus, from Nicholas of Cusa or his Greek antecedents, or whether they emerged by spontaneous generation makes little difference to us here. The time-spirit of which Bruno was only one exponent was abroad in the land, and poetic minds were responsive to the combination of philosophy, science, and poetry that Bruno welded into a whole.

As elsewhere in these essays, I shall employ a poet, rather than a scientist, as our guide to old ways of thinking, Henry More the Cambridge Platonist. Henry More was a poet at heart, but, unfortunately for his age, he had been denied the true poetic gift. Involved in language, more abstruse in his thinking than any of the metaphysicals, he is seldom worth the effort of decoding and deciphering. In an occasional lyric he wrote as a poet, and he had a real gift for satiric verse, but for the most part he was so conditioned by his youthful love of Spenser that he always sought to imitate his master, taking over Spenser's archaic words and constructions, allegorizing to such an extent that one needs a trail blazed by expositors to find a way through his "horrid wood." Yet he had a great deal of influence upon the younger generation of his time, both through his learned and complicated "Platonic Poems" and through his philosophical writings, most of all through his teaching. It is unfortunate that the greatest of the seven-

teenth-century "sons of More" published none of his poetry
in his own time. We shall find that son in Thomas Traherne,
who had the gift to express in poetry attitudes and ideas that I
believe he inherited from Henry More.

More was a Cambridge Platonist, with all the connotations
and contradictions that the word *Platonism* involved in the
seventeenth century. Like his fellow-student at Christ's College, John Milton, he read into Plato much that would have
surprised that philosopher. His Platonism was a fusion of
many sources: the mysticism of Pythagoras, the magic of
the Hermetic books, interpretations of Ficino, Pico della
Mirandola, Porphyry, most of all "Plotin," as he called Plotinus. His was the Platonism, too, of Kepler, by whose mysticism More was influenced. His God was the Deity of Plenitude, creating with lavish and unwithdrawing hand. But we
need not enter into these matters of philosophy and theology
in detail. One of the great appeals of Platonism to More
was that it afforded a philosophical basis for acceptance of
the new astronomy. Vestiges of the old astrology remain in
More's thinking, as in Milton's; he never lost his feeling for
the "true consent" of planet and element. Yet Platonism
could be made compatible with the Copernican and Galilean
astronomy, as with the expansion of the universe taught by
the Brunoesque philosophy. Indeed to Platonists like More—
as to Copernicus himself—the new astronomy was not new,
but a welcome return to cosmology earlier than that of
Ptolemy, taught by Pythagoras, Democritus, Leucippus, and
many others.

"I'll take my flight above this outward sunne," More
wrote in one of his Platonic poems, "Lift my self up in the
Theologie of heavenly Plato," and from that vantage point
contemplate the sun of Copernicus and Kepler:

> The archetype of this sunne, that bright Idee
> Of steddie Good, that doth his beames dilate
> Through all the worlds, all lives and beings propagate.

The Copernican world-system lent itself readily to Platonic analogues to More as to Kepler:

> The sunne's a type of that eternall light
> Which we call *God*, a fair delineament
> Of that which *Good* in Plato's school is hight,
> His *T'Agathon*, with beauteous rayes bedight.

> The *Intellectuall* sunne whose energies
> Are all things that appear in vitall light,
> Whose brightnesse passeth every creatures sight,
> Yet round about him stird with gentle fire
> All things do dance; their being, action, might,
> They thither do direct with strong desire,
> To embosome him with strong embracements they desire.
>
> (*Psychathanasia*, III.iii.10–12)

There is no one of Galileo's discoveries that More did not introduce into his Platonic poems "to show that Pythagore's position's right, Copernicks, or whosoever's dogma hight." Yet while the earlier More had accepted nearly all the premises from which Bruno reached his conclusions—the Copernican hypothesis, the neo-Pythagorean and neo-Platonic conception of plenitude—he did not at first accept the conception of infinite space, infinite time, and an infinity of worlds. Of all the cases of conversion to the full implications of the "new Philosophy," More's is one of the most interesting, because it occurred so suddenly and so completely. He set down some account of that conversion.

In the last stanzas of the *Psychathanasia*, one of his Platonic poems dealing with the immortality of the soul, he faced the issue and, while granting that he had approached close to ideas of eternity and infinity, he still denied the truth of these "ancient heresies." Yet, as he himself said, "I have sworn more faithfull friendship with Truth then with my self." Within a short space of time, he carried the premises to their conclusion and published a work that was at once a retraction and an affirmation, a long poem called *Democritus Platonissans, Or An Essay upon the Infinity of Worlds out of Platonick Principles*. "Roused up by a new Philosophick Furie," as he himself said, he denied "the Hypothesis of either the world or time being finite; defending the infinitude of both." Henry More still occupies a significant place in the history of philosophy because of his part in developing the metaphysics of *space* in the period between Descartes and Berkeley. His importance for my present purposes lies less in his metaphysics than in his response to what I have called the *aesthetics of infinity*.

The telescopic heavens enthralled rather than disturbed him. He did not feel with Donne that new astronomy had "disproportioned the pure form" of the heavens.

> Tell me therefore
> When you behold with your admiring eyes
> Heavens Canopie all to be spangled o're
> With sprinkled stars, what can you well devise
> Which causen may such carelesse order in the skies.[16]

Only to men who still believe in the earth as center and the heavens as canopy do the skies appear in "careless order." The old pattern had been made by men living in a finite universe, who, thinking of the stars from their finite point of view, had made them into artificial constellations. The fixed stars are not mere stars, twinkling in man's night-sky; they

[16] Henry More, *Infinity of Worlds*, in *Complete Poems*, ed. by Alexander Grosart (1878), stanza 53.

are suns, centers to other universes, as our sun to ours. Could we see the universe from the throne of God, "Numbers infinite of [worlds] would strike our 'stonished sight." Henry More did not doubt that other worlds were inhabited: the moon, the planets of our universe might all have their creatures,

> And what is done in this Terrestriall starre,
> The same is done in every Orb beside,   (Stanza 13)

The goodness of God had not been limited to one creation of one universe. Time was infinite, creation a continuing process:

> long ago there Earths have been
> Peopled with men and beasts before this Earth,
> And after this shall others be again
> And other beasts and other humane birth . . .
> Another Adam once received breath,
> And still another in endlesse repedation . . .   (Stanza 76)

Beyond and beyond our universe, stretching in space and time, are, were, and might be other worlds, filled with the creatures of God. Let man begin to understand the unbounded universe of which he is part and he will cease to talk about the "disorder" and the "disproportion" of the heavens, think rather in terms of new order and new proportion, new distances for which mathematicians and astronomers were only beginning a new language, and grasp in some small degree the extraordinary and astounding new harmony of the skies.

Religious philosopher that he was, Henry More created his infinite universe from the Infinite God in whom he believed, a God of plenitude, whose nature was to create to superabundance:

> Wherefore this precious sweet Ethereall dew
> For ought we know, God each where did distill,

And thorough all that hollow Vastnesse threw,
And the wide gaping drought therewith did fill,
His endlesse overflowing goodnesse spill
In every place; which streight he did contrive
Int' infinite severall worlds, as his best skill
Did him direct and creatures could receive:
For matter infinite needs infinite worlds must give . . .

And that even infinite such worlds there be,
That unexhausted Good that God is hight,
A full sufficient reason is to me,
Who simple Goodness make the highest Deity.

(Stanzas 50–51)

Such a Deity could not have created one world, one universe, once and once only; His world, His universe, His cosmos must reach to infinity, without limitation of time or space, must be as diverse, as full, as varied as its limitations would permit. Not for Henry More, generous and exuberant by nature, the Aristotelian Unmoved Mover, the Self-Sufficient who had no need for self-expression in creation. More's Deity was far more lavish than the Nature praised by Comus, expressing Himself not in the spawn of the sea and silkworms but in worlds unnumbered:

farre aboven,
Further then furthest thought of men can traverse,
Still are new worlds aboven and aboven,
In th' endlesse hollow Heaven, and each world hath his Sun.

(Stanza 59)

Important though his ideas of space were in the history of metaphysics, More's response to the vastness, grandeur, and magnificence of the universe was more often that of a poet than of a metaphysician. Space afforded him not only logical satisfaction but emotional gratification. His vocabulary is significant of a new attitude: as he surveys the astounding cosmos, his soul, "drunk with Divinitie" is "borne away above her usuall bounds" to delighted astonishment with the new infinity

> Of Time, of Worlds, of firie flaming Rounds:
> Which sight in sober mood my spirits quite confounds.
>
> (Stanza 72)

Excessive *vast* led to excessive emotion:

> th' infinite I'll sing
> Of Time, of Space . . . I'm brent
> With eager rage, my heart for joy doth spring
> And all my spirits move with pleasant trembeling.
>
> An inward triumph doth my soul up-heave
> And spread abroad through endlesse 'spersed air.
> My nimble mind this clammie clod doth leave,
> And lightly stepping on from starre to starre,
> Swifter then lightning, passeth wide and farre,
> Measuring th' unbounded Heavens and wastfull skie:
> Ne ought she finds her passage to debarre.
> For still the azure Orb as she draws nigh
> Gives back, new stars appear, the worlds walls 'fore her flie!
>
> (Stanzas 5–6)

His is a delight in vastness, an emotional response to something that arouses and fills the emotions to overflowing, that causes imagination to stretch its wings and take off into the vastly expanded universe, to delight in the fullness, the diversity, the richness of infinite space, filled with infinite worlds, the expression of a superabundant Deity, "the inexhausted Good that God is hight." His imagination expanded with the expansion of space. Exulting in spaciousness, he experienced an "enlarg'd delight" as "unbounded joys" filled his "boundlesse mind."

As Milton had no vocabulary for the vast illimitable ocean without bound, Henry More had none for the infinite universe. In his metaphysics, he transferred to Space some twenty adjectives and epithets that had formerly been applied only to Deity. The new universe made him "drunk with Divinitie," "brent with eager rage"; his "heart for joy doth spring"; his soul was exalted by "an inward triumph"; his "spirits move with pleasant trembeling." He exulted in the experience, yet he trembled with emotion compounded of delight and awe. A generation later men began to find words for such experience, responding with mingled pleasure and "trembeling" to the vast in the universe, later still to the vast in the world. Henry More had always loved beauty, but beauty had been associated in his mind with the finite, the limited, the proportioned. Beauty satisfied the emotions; it did not confound them. Infinity overwhelmed. In his conversion to infinity Henry More had had an experience he was never to forget. If he could not write as a poet, he felt as a poet, and felt something no poet before him had attempted to express. He was the first English poet who attempted to put into language man's feeling for what was not yet called Sublime—a Sublime which came from the "new Philosophy" that no longer called all in doubt, but rather released human imagination to a spaciousness of thought man had not known before. The Idea of Infinity had demolished the Circle of Perfection.

5

CONTENT AND ASPIRATION

"Shakespeare lived in a world of time, Milton in a universe of space." We have seen our ancestors standing between two worlds, an old animate world reflecting the macrocosm, reflected by the microcosm, and a new mechanistic world taking its way among the planets, responsive less to the Voice of God than to the Law of Nature. Yet never did they realize their dilemma more acutely than when they found themselves between an old world and a new universe, unintelligible in its "vast disproportions." For centuries man had lived in a world, like Shakespeare conscious of the universe only as the planets and stars affected his life. His world had been the center of the cosmic system, and he the center of a world made especially for him, the crown and summit of creation. "Man is ev'rything, and more," as Herbert said:

> For us the windes do blow;
> The earth doth rest, heav'n move, and fountains flow.
> Nothing we see but means our good;
> As our delight, or as our treasure;
> The whole is, either our cupboard of food,
> Or cabinet of pleasure.

Upon belief in this proud position man had built his metaphysics, his ethics and his aesthetics. No matter whether the world was still in appearance as on the day of Creation, no matter that he struggled with thorns and thistles, this was still the world that the Lord had made, man still the one creature He had created to love and serve Him.

The position of the earth had changed. The heavens no longer declared eternal and immutable values. Gone was Nature's nest of concentric boxes, evidence of permanence and stability, gone even more the supreme proof of limitation— the limits of the universe. The great circles were broken, the universe dispersed into a nebulous infinity that had no shape or pattern. The moon was a world; each planet in our system was a world. They had their mountains and their seas, perhaps their men. Not only that, but

> farre aboven,
> Further then furthest thought of men can traverse,
> Still are new worlds, aboven and still aboven,
> In th' endlesse hollow Heaven, and each World hath his Sun.

Perhaps each of those far-flung cosmic worlds gave birth to men—living creatures in profusion, existing from eternity to infinity, beings in comparison with whom the sinful sons of Adam were little higher than beasts in the field, birds on the wing, even mites that only new "optick glasses" could discover. Faced with a new universe, thoughtful man must do one of two things: deny such man-made hypotheses and take refuge in the faith of his fathers; or accept them and begin again where Adam had begun to frame his aesthetics, his ethics, his metaphysics by a new appeal to Nature, as he rethought the world and the universe from which he deduced them.

Fontenelle amusingly suggested the dilemma of our ancestors. In his *Conversations upon a Plurality of Worlds*, a

Philosopher, strolling with a Lady in the moonlight between the close-clipped hedges of a formal garden, taught the new cosmology to his apt pupil, who was at once enthralled and appalled by the discoveries of new science and new philosophy. When after the last evening's conversation, she had grasped some sense of the new universe, she spoke for many of her contemporaries of both sexes:

You have made the Universe so large, *says she*, that I know not where I am, or what will become of me; what, is it all to be divided into heaps confusedly, one among another? Is every Star the Center of a Vortex, as big as ours? Is that vast space which comprehends our Sun and Planets, but an inconsiderable part of the Universe? And are there as many spaces, as there are fix'd Stars? I protest it is dreadful.

But the Philosopher was one of those who delighted in the freedom of the new space, whose imagination expanded.with the vast:

Dreadful, Madame, *said I;* I think it very pleasant; when the Heavens were a little blue Arch, stuck with Stars, methought the Universe was too strait and close, and I was almost stifled for want of Air; but now it is enlarg'd in heighth and breadth, and a thousand and a thousand Vortex's taken in, I begin to breathe with more freedom and think the Universe to be incomparably more magnificent than it was before. Nature hath spared no cost, even to profuseness, and nothing can be so glorious, as to see such a prodigious number of Vortex's, whose several centers are possess'd by a particular Sun.[1]

One group of our seventeenth-century ancestors—if I may use modern psychological idiom—had suffered from agoraphobia, another from claustrophobia. Fearful of the vast, the

---

[1] *A Plurality of Worlds, translated into English by Mr. Glanvill* (London, 1702), pp. 128-29.

unlimited, the unpatterned, the first were at home in Cowley's "very little House," asking no more than Herbert's "cupboards of food" for sustenance and "cabinets of pleasure" for diversion. Bounded in a nutshell, they welcomed their bonds. Others had been restless in their "well furnisht tents." They were by nature kings of infinite space, but their thoughts that wandered through eternity had never before had space in which to expand. Since men have always been by nature classicists and romanticists, each temperament responded to the vastness of the new universe as might be expected.

I

In his response to the "new Philosophy" Donne, as we have seen, was a modern. His contemporary Shakespeare, who lived on, like Donne, into a world of telescopes and stars and expanded space, remained an Elizabethan. Shakespeare must have seen the "new star" in 1604, must have heard of Galileo's discoveries of 1610, "of which all corners were full." He was writing some of his greatest plays during the period of Donne's transformation from Elizabethan to modern. Yet his poetic imagination showed no more response to new stars or a new universe than to the Copernican theory. As Caroline Spurgeon's analysis of his images indicates, his imagination was not stirred by concepts far removed from men's experience. "His feet are firmly set upon 'this goodly frame, the earth,' his eyes are focussed on the daily life around him." He was much more interested in man than in the universe. Only in *King Lear*, written at the time his contemporaries were dwelling upon the dramatic new star of 1604, did his mind seem to concern itself particularly with cosmology, and here his interest was not in astronomy but in the "dire por-

tents," troubled heavens and planets of astrology. Disruption
in the heavens presaged disruption upon earth, the storms of
the geocosm paralleled those in the microcosm, but our attention and Shakespeare's is on Lear, the man, rather than on the
world and the universe. Shakespeare ceased writing at the
very time that the "new Philosophy" called all in doubt to his
contemporary poet. Was that, I wonder, mere coincidence, or
did Shakespeare, who always had his finger upon the pulse of
his time, deliberately retire to a simpler life from a world and
universe that were growing unintelligible?

The Elizabethan dramatist whose imagination would have
responded most sensitively to the new astronomy died too
early to know much of it. Had he lived, Christopher Marlowe might today preempt the place accorded by modern
literary historians to John Donne, as the first English poet
who grasped the implications of the new celestial discoveries.
And I venture to suggest—since one may comfortably surmise about the dead—that to Marlowe the "new Philosophy" would not have called all in doubt. Miss Spurgeon's
study of his dominant images has led to this conclusion:

This imaginative preoccupation with the dazzling heights and vast
spaces of the universe is, together with a magnificent surging upward thrust and aspiration, the dominating note of Marlowe's
mind. He seems more familiar with the starry courts of heaven
than with the green fields of earth, and he loves rather to watch
the movements of meteors and planets than to study the faces of
men. No matter what he is describing, the pictures he draws tend
to partake of this celestial and magnificent quality.

Not even the later poets better set the note of aspiration than
did Marlowe in *Tamburlaine:*

    Nature, that fram'd us of foure Elements,
    Warring within our breasts for regiment,
    Doth teach us all to have aspyring minds:

Our soles, whose faculties can comprehend
The wondrous Architecture of the world,
And measure every wandering planets course,
Still climbing after knowledge infinite,
And alwaies moving, as the restless Spheares,
Will us to weare our selves and never rest.

Tamburlaine's own goal, to be sure, was "the sweet fruition of an earthly crown," but one of Doctor Faustus' first demands of Mephistopheles was for "a booke where I might see all characters and planets of the heavens, that I might know their motions and dispositions." In his absence, the Chorus said,

Learned Faustus
To know the secrets of Astronomy,
Graven in the booke of Jove his firmament,
Did mount himself to scale Olympus top . . .
He now is gone to prove Cosmography.

The creator of Faustus would have welcomed the new discoveries of a new philosophy, as the creator of Tamburlaine, had he lived long enough, might have added still another sequel, a cosmic voyage in which he sent his insatiable conqueror to ride in triumph through other worlds than ours. Optimism rather than pessimism, exultation instead of despondency would, I believe, have been the early note of the poetry of the "new Philosophy" in England had Marlowe lived to ripeness.

There were many who denied the heresies of the new astronomy as their fathers had denied the truth of the Copernican hypothesis. Others questioned even though they could not deny. Both groups were as conscious of the dilemma in which they had been placed and as vocal as those who welcomed the new truths. The arguments of the traditionalists were various. The new truths were not true at all; they were far-fetched hypotheses invented by man, who, incapable of knowing himself, presumptuously strove to comprehend the universe:

> Man! foolish man!
> Scarce knowst thou how thyself began;
> Scarce hast thou thought enough to prove thou art;
> Yet steel'd with studied boldness, thou dar'st try
> To send thy doubting reason's dazzled eye
> Through the mysterious gulf of vast immensity.[2]

"Canst thou loose the bands of Orion?" asked the voice from the whirlwind. Modern man in his insolence would order the planets, command heaven itself:

> of Meridians and Parallels,
> Man hath weav'd out a net, and this net throwne
> Upon the Heavens, and now they are his owne.
> Loth to goe up the hill, or labour thus
> To goe to heaven, we make heaven come to us.
> We spur, we reine the starres, and in their race
> They're diversely content t' obey our pace.[3]

Even were the new theories true, declared others, man need not attempt to comprehend them nor be fearful; the spacious universe on high is God's concern, not man's:

> Were worlds as many as the rays which stream
> From heaven's bright eyes, or madding wits do dream,
> They would not reel in nought, nor wand'ring stray,
> But draw to thee, who could their centres stay.[4]

God did not prohibit man from pondering the meaning of this vast new universe; Milton's Angel said to Adam:

[2] Matthew Prior, *I Am That I Am.*
[3] Donne, *First Anniversary*, ll.278–84.
[4] Drummond of Hawthornden, *Hymn of the Fairest Fair.*

> To ask or search I blame thee not; for Heaven
> Is as the Book of God before thee set,
> Wherein to read his wondrous works, and learn
> His seasons, hours, or days, or months, or years.
>
> (PL, VIII.66–69)

But man must not concern himself unduly over such matters: "whether Heaven move or Earth / Imports not, if thou reckon right." No matter what the appeal to intellectual curiosity—and Milton did not deny that appeal—Raphael's final lesson to Adam was ethical rather than scientific or metaphysical:

> Heaven is for thee too high
> To know what passes there. Be lowly wise;
> Think only what concerns thee and thy being;
> Dream not of other worlds, what creatures there
> Live, in what state, condition, or degree—
> Contented that thus far hath been revealed
> Not of Earth only, but of highest Heaven.
>
> (PL, VIII.172–78)

Here is one theme of limitation. But Milton, as we shall see, stood on a middle ground between the poets who preached content and the "soaring souls that sailed among the spheres," to whom the new universe taught a lesson of never-ceasing aspiration.

The classical poets loved the ethical limitation and perfection of the circle as they loved the restraint of the epigram or sonnet:

> In small proportions we just beauties see;
> And in short measures life may perfect be.

Donne, capable of both moods, sometimes felt the value of a proportion that the limitations of poetry might impose on disproportioned emotions, as he implied in *The Triple Foole:*

> I thought, if I could draw my paines,
> Through Rimes vexation, I should them allay.
> Griefe brought to numbers cannot be so fierce,
> For, he tames it, that fetters it in verse.

In *The Canonization* the poet who often broke the pattern praised it:

> As well a well wrought urne becomes
> The greatest ashes, as half-acre tombes.

"To enclose Infinite riches in a little room"—this has always been the greatness of classical art, as restraint, proportion and moderation are the ideals of classical ethics. We have seen the consistency between Marvell's feeling for the dew-drop mirroring the macrocosm, the "perfect hemisphere" of the low hill at Billbarrow, the architectural proportion of Appleton House, and the ethical lesson implied by all of them:

> But all things are composed here
> Like Nature, orderly and near;
> In which we the Dimensions find
> Of that more sober Age and Mind,
> When larger-sized Men did stoop
> To enter at a narrow loop;
> As practising in doors so strait,
> To strain themselves through Heavens Gate. . . .
>
> Humility alone designs
> Those short but admirable lines,
> By which, ungirt and unconstrain'd,
> Things greater are in less contain'd.

Such poets had no desire to break the bounds which they had built for their own restraint. A little was enough for their regulated minds. "Too much," as one of them said, "craves more." *Nothing in excess:* "too much" led to discontent, dissatisfaction, pessimism.

"What is man in the Infinite?" questioned Pascal. "A Nothing in comparison with the All; an All in comparison with Nothing. . . . equally incapable of seeing the Nothing from which he came, and the Infinite in which he is swallow'd up." For centuries *infinite* had been God's word, not man's. But now man was beginning to apply to an expanded universe adjectives and epithets long reserved for Deity, appropriate alone to the Incomprehensible:

> Whose depths, beneath the centre, none can sound,
> Whose heights, 'bove heav'n and thoughts so lofty soar,
> Whose breadth no feet, no lines, no chains, no eyes survey,
> Whose lengths no bounds can reach, no worlds can bound.[5]

It would not have surprised the poets of limitation to know that before the end of the century, Space was to become not only the "Sensorium of Deity" but Deity itself. In their own minds was no such confusion, or logical contradiction. Leave to faith those things that are faith's, they urged; among those must be omnipresence, immeasurability, incomprehensibility. "Look to me, Faith, and look to my Faith, God," Donne wrote in his "Elegie for Prince Henry," reminding himself that man's concern was with "Quotidian things, and / Equidistant hence, / Shut in for Men in one Circumference." God might transcend the Circle; His alone were

> th' enormous Greatnesses, which are
> So disproportion'd and so angulare,
> As is God's Essence, Place, and Providence.

[5] Phineas Fletcher, *Immensity of God.*

Man could not understand heights and depths; even the angels saw God only when "dark with excessive bright His skirts appear." Man could seek to understand Him only in aspects in which He limited his vastness. Before the Word he stood in awe; but he might love the Word made Flesh:

> O little all; in thy embrace
> The World lies warm, and likes its place.[6]

Enraptured with the small, in which the great was epitomized, they loved the symbol of the Infant, "Immensity cloyster'd in thy dear wombe":

> Though the expanded firmament
> Was for thee a narrow tent,
> In thy wombe thou wouldst be pent.[7]

"Welcome to our wondering sight," wrote Crashaw in his *Hymn of the Nativity,*

> Eternity shut in a span!
> Summer in Winter! Day in Night!
> Heaven in Earth! and God in Man!
> Great, little one; whose all-embracing Birth
> Lifts Earth to Heaven, stoops heaven to Earth.

Quarles drew the "Emblem" of a too-aspiring generation in his picture of "A Cupid trying in vain to grasp a Globe in his arms":

> Oh, how our widen'd arms can over-stretch
> Their own dimensions! How our hands can reach
> Beyond their distance! How our yielding breast
> Can shrink to be more full and full possest
> Of this inferior orb! . . .
> We gape, we grasp, we gripe, add store to store;
> Enough requires too much; too much craves more. . . .

---

[6] Crashaw, *In the Glorious Epiphanie of our Lord God.*
[7] Nathaniel Wanley, *The Obligation,* in *Scintullulae Sacrae.*

> Thus we, poor little worlds! with blood and sweat,
> In vain attempt to comprehend the great.   (*Emblems*, ii.2)

Insatiable men were attempting to make time into Eternity, to expand a finite world into Infinity. Across their rhapsodies about the brave new universe came the warning voice of the past: time must end, and the world must end.

> They which dream
> An everlastingness in worlds vast frame,
> Think well some region where they dwell may wrack,
> But that the whole nor time nor force can shake,

yet the omens foretold the destruction of their new world, as of the world of the past. "Frantic," they would "see heaven's stately lights, / Like drunkards, wayless reel amidst their heights." On the Day of Judgment they would learn the irony of the lesson they taught. In despair they would seek the Heaven they had destroyed, only to find it gone:

> As more and more the warning signs increase,
> Wild dread deprives lost Adam's race of peace;
> From out their granddam Earth they fain would fly,
> But whither know not, heavens are far and high.

The earth must end. The poets of limitation asked only that Heaven remain.

> In dust now must our greatness buried lie,
> Yet is it comfort with the world to die.[8]

II

Of all the religious poets of the seventeenth century, none more consistently taught the happiness of limitation and restraint than did George Herbert. *The Pulley* and *The Col-*

---

[8] This and the preceding quotations are from Drummond, *The Shadow of Judgment*, in *Flowers of Sion*.

lar are not, I think, his most characteristic verse, though they have been made to seem so by anthologists who overstress the metaphysical wit of the century. If Herbert struggled in his search for God, he attained peace in finding Him. His "works" might well be called by that word reiterated in so many of them—"content." Never was man more willing to accept the limitations of a finite world and a finite universe than he who wrote:

> This soul doth span the world, and hang content
>> From either pole unto the centre:
> Where in each room of the well furnisht tent,
>> He lies warm, and without adventure   (*Content*)

Herbert had followed the progress of the new science; what member of his distinguished family had not? Perhaps, like Donne and many other contemporaries, he too had gone through a period of "Hydroptique and immoderate love of learning." But, as he destroyed his worldly poetry, he put aside the restlessness of the too-inquiring mind when he found peace in the life of a country clergyman. "I know the wayes of Learning," he wrote

>> what the starres conspire,
> What willing nature speaks, what forc'd by fire;
> Both th' old discoveries, and the new-found seas,
> The stock and surplus, cause and historie:
> All these stand open, or I have the keyes:
>> Yet I love thee.   (*The Pearl*)

From books he learned what men called "great" discoveries, but he could smile at such greatness, as John Donne had laughed at the exaggeration of Thomas Coryat's "extraordinary" discoveries in his *Crudities:*

> Oh to what heighth will love of greatnesse drive
> Thy leavened spirit, *Sesqui-superlative?*

Venice vast lake thou hadst seen, and wouldst seek then
Some vaster thing . . .

What men considered great and vast in the world had no
appeal for Herbert who had discovered the truly vast things
with which man need concern himself:

> Philosophers have measur'd mountains,
> Fathom'd the depths of seas, of states, and kings,
> Walk'd with a staffe to heav'n, and trac'd fountains:
>   But there are two vast, spacious things,
> The which to measure it doth more behove:
> Yet few there are that sound them—Sinne and Love.
>   (*The Agonie*)

Herbert knew astronomy, old and new. He was as familiar as any of his contemporaries "with Centric and Eccentric scribl'd o'er, Cycle and Epicycle, orb in orb," but the
"Eccentrique parts" did not "disproportion that pure forme"
to him, nor did he share the passion of his age for restraining
the stars and planets in their courses by man-made laws. He
wrote:

> As men, for fear the starres should sleep and nod,
>   And trip at night, have spheres suppli'd;
> As if a starre were duller then a clod,
>   Which knows his way without a guide. . . .
>
> Then burn thy Epicycles, foolish man;
>   Burn all thy spheres, and save thy head.
> Faith needs no staffe of flesh, but stoutly can
>   To heav'n alone both go, and leade.   (*Divinitie*)

He dismissed the "fleet Astronomer," the "nimble Diver,"
and the "subtle Chymick," who sought to explain the mysteries of things:

> The fleet Astronomer can bore,
> And thred the spheres with his quick-piercing minde;
> He views their stations, walks from doore to doore,
>   Surveys, as if he had design'd
> To make a purchase there: he sees their dances,
>   And knoweth long before
> Both their full-ey'd aspects, and secret glances   (*Vanitie*)

Astronomer, diver, chemist had discovered secrets in the limbec, in the depths of ocean, in the heavens. "What hath not man sought out and found, / But his deare God?"

The new expanded heavens did not stir his imagination to take wing and fly up into the ether; for a moment he shared Pascal's terror of the eternal silence of infinite space, when he wrote:

> Although there were some fourtie heav'ns, or more,
>   Sometimes I peere above them all;
> Sometimes I hardly reach a score,
>   Sometimes to hell I fall.
>
> O rack me not to such a vast extent;
>   Those distances belong to thee:
> The world's too little for thy tent,
>   A grave too big for me.   (*The Temper, I*)

From his one imaginary voyage into space, Herbert willingly returned to earth which, whatever its place in the cosmic scheme, remained the center of his universe. The world and the universe might be threatened by scientists and philosophers, the circles broken, but man was all symmetry, "full of proportions one limb to another, and all to all the world besides." For man the winds *did* blow, earth rest, heaven move, and fountains flow. The world and the universe were still made for him. "More creatures wait on man than he'll take notice of,"

Of all the creatures both in sea and land,
Onely to Man thou hast made known thy wayes,
And put the penne alone into his hand,
And made him Secretarie of thy Praise. . . .
Man is the worlds high Priest. (*Providence*)

He felt none of the restlessness of that type of man who was
never satisfied:

Now he will fight it out, and to the warres;
Now eat his bread in peace,
And snudge in quiet; now he scorns increase;
Now all day spares. (*Giddinesse*)

To giddy men, avid for novelty, restive beneath restraint, he
spoke of the quiet mind, of contentment with limitation, and
of the happiness of one who in his "well-furnisht tent" lay
warm, and without adventure:

Mark how the fire in flints doth quiet lie,
Content and warm t' it self alone:
But when it would appeare to others eye,
Without a knock it never shone.

Give me the pliant minde, whose gentle measure
Complies and suits with all estates;
Which can let loose to a crown, and yet with pleasure
Take up within a cloisters gate. (*Content*)

To a generation that sought to break down the walls of the
world and the walls of the universe in which man had long
dwelt comfortably, and to make in the image of their own
restless minds a boundless universe, void of pattern and form,
he wrote of the vanity of believing that true values ever lay
in mere size:

Content thee, greedie heart.
Modest and moderate joyes to those, that have

Title to more hereafter, when they part,
　　Are passing brave . . .

Wherefore sit down, good heart;
Grasp not at much, for fear thou losest all. . . .

Then close again the seam,
Which thou hast open'd: do not spread thy robe
In hope of great things. Call to minde thy dream,
　　　　An earthly globe,
On whose meridian was engraven,
These seas are tears, and heav'n the haven.　　　(*The Size*)

III

Between religious poets like Herbert, who found shelter
from the incomprehensible universe in faith, and another
group of aspiring souls "still climbing after knowledge infinite," were many who, refusing to accept the metaphysics
of a new philosophy, nevertheless experienced an aesthetic
gratification in the vast. On this middle ground stood Milton.
Philosophically he denied the major tenets of eternity and
infinity, as theologically he denied the God of Plenitude. Milton's official Deity, as Adam realized, was the Aristotelian
Self-Sufficient:

Thou in thyself art perfect, and in Thee
Is no deficience found. . . . No need that thou
Shouldst propagate, already infinite,
And through all numbers absolute, though One.
　　　　　　　　　　　　(*PL*, VIII.415–21)

But Adam had added: "Not so is Man." And not so was Milton, on one side of his nature at least. Whether because of

his youthful training in debate and rhetoric, or because of a natural balance of his "elements," the young Milton responded equally to opposites: day and night, light and shade, *L'Allegro* and *Il Penseroso*. The Nature of Comus was like the nature of the Platonic Deity, profuse, superabundant, ubiquitous:

> Wherefore did Nature pour her bounties forth
> With such a full and unwithdrawing hand,
> Covering the earth with odours, fruits and flocks,
> Thronging the seas with spawn innumerable . . .
> And set to work millions of spinning worms,
> That in their green shops weave the smooth-haired silk
> To deck her sons?   (*Comus*, ll. 710–17)

The Lady replied with a mild ethical socialism, mingled with the classical doctrine of *nothing too much*. Her Nature taught restraint and limitation. If all good things were equally divided, there would be enough for all but no excess:

> She, good cateress,
> Means her provision only to the good,
> That live according to her sober laws
> And holy dictate of spare Temperance. (*Comus*, ll. 764–67)

The Lady won the debate, but the poet gave himself away: Comus's are by far the more persuasive speeches.

When in maturity Milton returned to the same "appeal to Nature for standards," the sea-spawn and the silkworms of *Comus* had become the heavens of the new astronomy, and Milton still swung between a Nature that taught restraint and limitation and one that expressed herself in profusion and superabundance:

> reasoning, I oft admire
> How Nature, wise and frugal, could commit

> Such disproportions, with superfluous hand
> So many nobler bodies to create,
> Greater to manifold, to this one use. . . . (*PL*, VIII.25–29)

So Adam to the Angel. No matter what the lesson of the dialogue on astronomy, Milton again gave himself away. Why introduce the passage at all at this important point in the argument unless the new astronomy *was* important to man, whatever he decided about it? And why develop it in so much detail? Would the Angel have permitted man to discourse at such length, unless Adam's creator, too, had felt the fascination of cosmology? Raphael might have answered Adam much more shortly, indeed might peremptorily have ordered him to put aside vain questions. Yet he said sympathetically, "To ask or search I blame thee not." Not only did he reply to each of Adam's points in detail but he added little lectures on themes Adam had not raised—new ideas which must have stirred Adam's curiosity even more. Milton's sources are familiar to us.[9] He had turned to John Wilkins, one of the leaders in the new science, for the basis of Adam's speeches, to Alexander Rosse, one of the most crusted conservatives of the day, for Raphael's. But while Milton awarded the palm to Raphael, as earlier to the Lady, he elevated both sources to poetry which, taken from its context, might well make its author seem one of the "soaring souls" who felt the spell of a new vast cosmic nature: "this Earth a spot, a grain, / An atom with the Firmament compared"; "spaces incomprehensible, (for such their distance argues and their swift return Diurnal"; "such vast room in Nature unpossessed / By living soul, desert and desolate"; "and other

[9] Grant McColley, in "Milton's Dialogue of Astronomy," *PMLA*, LII (1937), 728–62, has shown that Adam's speeches are based upon a work by John Wilkins, the Angel's upon one of Alexander Rosse.

Suns, perhaps, / With their attendant Moons, thou wilt descry, / Communicating male and female light, / Which two great sexes animate the World." Some of these phrases are Adam's, some Raphael's; emotionally there is no difference. It was the Angel not Adam, whose mind played with the idea of a world in the moon—"if land be there, / Fields and inhabitants"—the Angel, too, who suggested the possibility of other suns and other moons, and told Adam of the grandeur of "Heaven's wide circuit," which speaks "the Maker's high magnificence, who built / So spacious, and his line stretched out so far."

Satisfied with the Angel's explanation, Adam returned to cultivate his garden, in which he might have found an epitome of the problem that had engaged his mind in the larger world of the macrocosm. "God Almighty first planted a garden," said Bacon. Did God's Garden of Eden show the limitation or the profusion of Nature?

> Flowers worthy of Paradise, which not nice Art
> In beds and curious knots, but Nature boon
> Poured forth profuse on hill, and dale, and plain. . . .
>
> (*PL*, IV.241–43)
>
> A wilderness of sweets; for Nature here
> Wantoned as in her prime, and played at will
> Her virgin fancies, pouring forth more sweet,
> Wild above rule or art, enormous bliss.   (*PL*, V.294–97)

Perhaps Adam's "studious mind abstruse" had not pondered on the contrast between the Nature in his garden and "Nature wise and frugal." But Eve, busy as she was, knew all about the "nature" of gardens. She said:

> "Adam, well may we labour still to dress
> This Garden, still to tend plant, herb, and flowers,

> Our pleasant work enjoined; but, till more hands
> Aid us, the work under our labour grows,
> Luxurious by restraint; what we by day
> Lop overgrown, or prune, or prop, or bind,
> One night or two with wanton growth derides,
> Tending to wild."   (*PL*, IX.205–12)

Nature's garden was wild, luxuriant, excessive, profuse. Upon it Adam and Eve imposed limitation and restraint, pruning its luxuriance, improving not only upon Nature but presumably upon God. Here are two persistent aspects of Milton's personality, one satisfied with proportion and limitation, the other revelling in the luxuriant and the unrestrained. His classical and religious training led him to an ethics of moderation in which he sincerely believed. He himself, however, charmingly suggested the other side of the picture in *Tetrachordon,* when after a dissertation on the hard labor of attaining wisdom, he wrote: "We cannot therefore alwayes be contemplative, or pragmatically abroad but have need of some delightful intermissions, wherein the enlarg'd soul may leave off a while her severe schooling; and like a glad youth in wandring vacancy, may keep her hollidaies to joy and harmless pastime." [10]

In the astronomy of *Paradise Lost* Milton, whether or not he realized it, broke the Circle of Perfection. Officially Adam's world was still a Ptolemaic or a Tychonic universe, the earth in the center, the planets following circular courses. This was Adam's universe, but it was not always his creator's. Milton sent Satan on a journey through old Chaos and old Elements, yet on his journey Satan passed by Galileo's moon

[10] H. V. S. Ogden discussed the passage and Milton's dual attitude in "Variety and Contrast in 17th Century Aesthetics," *Journal of the History of Ideas,* X (1949), 159–82.

and pondered the possibility of inhabitants of other planetary worlds. With the golden Compasses Milton's Christ circumscribed a Ptolemaic universe, yet the two great celestial bodies that shone at His command were Galileo's sun and moon; the planet Venus showed Galilean phases; and Christ returned in glory to the Father over Galileo's Milky Way. Milton denied the infinity of the world, denied the metaphysics of space that was developing powerfully in the period of his major poems, yet he responded to the aesthetics of the new space as fully as any poet of his century. Some years ago I suggested that, while Shakespeare still lived in a world of time, Milton's imagination traveled through a universe of space. Years have deepened that impression in my mind. Satan's voyage through Chaos is one of the great cosmic voyages of a period that sent imaginary mariners to the moon and planets in search of other worlds and other men. Milton's canvas in *Paradise Lost* is the vastest used by an English artist. Nowhere among the poets who praised the new universe do we find more majestic suggestions of the vastness of space than in the "cosmic perspectives" of a blind poet, whose framework was still the old finite universe. With "the Almighty Father from above" we bend down our eyes, "His own works and their works at once to view." With Satan we stand at Hell-Gates to see a scene for which Milton could find only a negative vocabulary, a vast illimitable ocean, without bound, where length and breadth and height and time and place are lost. Looking down "with wonder at the sudden view / Of all this World at once," we survey with Satan

> from eastern point
> Of Libra to the fleecy star that bears
> Andromeda far-off Atlantic seas,
> Beyond the horizon; then from pole to pole

He views his breadth,—and without longer pause,
Down right into the World's first region throws
His flight precipitant, and winds with ease
Through the vast marble air his oblique way
Amongst innumerable stars that shon,
Stars distant, but night-hand seemed other worlds.
Or other worlds they seemed, or happy isles.

(PL, III.557–66)

Ethically a poet of content and limitation, Milton the artist felt aesthetic gratification in the new vastness which as metaphysician he did not accept. He denied the idea of infinity. His universe in *Paradise Lost* is not infinite, yet it is indefinite, immense, and majestic. Like his own Archangel, Milton stood "betwixt the world destroyed and world restored."

IV

"I can love both faire and browne," said Donne, who could also turn at will from praise of the well-wrought urn and the "pretty room" of the sonnet to write in *Variety*:

The heavens rejoyce in motion, why should I
Abjure my so much lov'd variety? . . .
Pleasure is none, if not diversifi'd . . .
All things doe willingly in change delight,
The fruitful mother of our appetite.

Like Donne in his way and Milton in his, many of the seventeenth-century poets swung between the extremes of "content" and "aspiration," feeling now one, now the other. Some went all the way in their journeys into space. Burton may serve as their guide. "As a long-winged hawk . . . mounts aloft, and for his pleasure fetcheth many a circuit in the air, still soaring higher and higher, till he come to his full pitch," he wrote in the "Digression of Air" in the *Anatomy of Melancholy*, "so will I, having now come at last into these ample fields of air, wherein I may freely expatiate and exercise myself for my recreation, a while rove, wander round about the world, mount aloft to those ethereal orbs and celestial spheres, and so descend to my former elements again." Rising on wings, Burton's hawk scans the heavens, dips down to the bowels of the earth, mounts again to lunar and solar regions, pauses to consider whether the planets are inhabited, flies in imagination beyond the bounds of the known cosmic system to wonder whether, indefinitely or infinitely, there are other worlds, other planets, other cosmic universes in the new macrocosm of "these Copernical giants."

On his journey the long-winged hawk observed the picture of the heavens as they now seemed to man—heavens without form or order, no longer the familiar patterned night-skies:

How comes or wherefore is this *temeraria siderum dispositio,* this rash placing of stars, or as Epicurus will, *fortuita,* or accidental? Why are some big, some little, why are they so confusedly, unequally situated in the heavens, and set so much out of order? In all other things nature is equal, proportionable, and constant. . . . Why are the heavens so irregular? . . . whence is this difference? [11]

Disorder where order had been, irregularity in the celestial design into which generations of men had read patterns of artificial constellations—this was one aesthetic dilemma posed by the new astronomy. If, as man had believed, the heavens were intended as a canopy for his world, why had the compass of the Great Geometer not arranged the stars in neat

[11] *Anatomy of Melancholy*, II.ii, Mem. 3, p. 249.

concentric patterns? Thomas Burnet put the matter graphically in the *Sacred Theory of the Earth:*

Who can reckon up the Stars of the Galaxy, or direct us in the Use of them? And can we believe that those and all the rest were made for us? Of those few Stars that we enjoy, or that are visible to the Eye, there is not a tenth Part that is really useful to man; and no doubt, if the principal End of them had been our Pleasure or Conveniency, they would have been put in some better Order in respect of the Earth. They lie carelessly scatter'd, as if they had been sown in the Heaven, like Seed, by handfuls; and not by a Skilful Hand neither.

What a beautiful Hemisphere they would have made, if they had been plac'd in Rank and Order; if they had all been dispos'd into regular Figures, and the little ones set with due Regard to the greater, then all finisht, and made up into one fair Piece of that great Composition, according to the Rules of Art and Symmetry; what a surprizing Beauty this would have been to the Inhabitants of the Earth? What a lovely Roof to our little World? This indeed might have given one some Temptation to have thought that they had been made all for us.[12]

Henry More had written in more homely metaphor:

> A peck of peasen rudely poured out
> On plaister flore, from hasty heedlesse hond,
> Which lie all carelesse scattered about,
> To sight do in as seemly order stond,
> As those fair glistering lights in heaven are found.
> If only for this world they were intended,
> Nature would have adorn'd this azure Round
> With better Art, and easily have mended
> This harsh disorder'd order, and more beauty lended.
>
> (*Infinity of Worlds*, stanza 54)

[12] *Sacred Theory of the Earth* (6th ed.; London, 1726), I.II.xi.436–37.

"Beauty's best, proportion, is dead," said Donne, confused before the irregular heavens from which man could no longer deduce the old aesthetics. Later spirits faced disproportion gallantly, beginning to find delight in the disorder of the stars, as Herrick in the "sweet disorder" of a lovely woman:

> A sweet disorder in the dress
> Kindles in clothes a wantonness:—
> A lawn about the shoulders thrown
> Into a fine distraction, . . .
> A winning wave, deserving note,
> In the tempestuous petticoat,—
> A careless shoe-string, in whose tie
> I see a wild civility,—
> Do more bewitch me, than when art
> Is too precise in every part.

If there may be charm in a careless yet lovely woman, how much more bewitching the "wild civility" of a hoydenish Nature? The artist could still find standards in an appeal to Nature, even when Nature had changed. As Henry More said:

> The meaner mind works with more nicetie,
> As Spiders wont to weave their idle web,
> But braver spirits do all things gallantly,
> Of lesser failings nought at all affred:
> > So Natures carelesse pencill dipt in light
> > With sprinkled starres hath spattered the Night.
> > > (*Cupid's Conflict*)

Perhaps Nature was tired of the constant attention to exquisite art she had known so long in her "narrow ingines." Wearied by repetition of the circle and the regular solids, Nature might break the laws she herself had imposed and express her prodigal personality in the "thousand thousand stars," letting her careless pencil have its way, and—we may surmise—splashing at ten-league canvasses with brushes of comets' hair. Or perhaps man felt the heavens irregular and disproportionate merely because he still thought in antiquated terms of his earth as the center, still believed that the sun and moon were created only to lighten his darkness. Enthusiastically the apostles of the new science found arguments to prove that only narrow minds could desire to believe that all things in the world and universe had been created for man. Little by little, men were turning from the glory of the earth to the greater glory of the God of a new universe, a vaster, grander, more majestic God than the Deity of their fathers. "Leave Mortality's low sphere," urged Cowley in *The Exstasy*:

> Ye Winds and Clouds, come lift me high,
> And on your airy pinions bear
> Swift through the regions of the sky. . . .
> And lo! How wide a space of air
> Extends new prospects to my eye!

In so far as his finite limitations permit, let man take a universal rather than a terrestrial view, and think of the universe not from a selfish center, but, with cosmic perspective, from the throne of God. Then he would find not "harsh disorder" but new order, an Order transcending in magnificence the old familiar pattern of the skies. Then his imagination and his soul, experiencing no limitation of time and space, may grow to greatness with the Great.

"Contentment is a sleepy thing!" cried Thomas Traherne, and so the poets of aspiration felt. To those who bade them to be content with the old world, they replied:

While you a spot of Earth possess with Care
Below the notice of the Geographer,
    I by the Freedom of my Soul,
      Possess, nay more, enjoy the whole:
To the Universe a claim I lay.[13]

One world was not enough. "One little world or two," wrote
Crashaw, "Alas! will never doe. We must have store."
Crashaw was thinking of the insatiability of the religious soul
in its search for God, but his contemporaries, using the same
terms, were seeking other cosmic worlds to conquer. " 'Tis
mean Ambition to define / A single World," wrote Traherne,

      To many I aspire,
    Tho one upon another hurl'd:
Nor will they all, if they be all confin'd
      Delight my Mind.

This busy, vast, enquiring Soul
    Brooks no Controul:
      'Tis very curious too,
Each one of all these Worlds must be
Enricht with infinite Variety
      And Worth; or 'twill not do.   (*Insatiableness, I*)

One world was not enough. Even one universe would not do
for the insatiable. The aspiring poets took wing and mounted
up into ether with their prose-companions, the cosmic voy-
agers, who set off in strange space-ships to discover a world
in the moon or the planets. Beyond our universe they sent
their imaginations into endless space in search of endless universes. Exulting in the fullness and diversity of a universe "so
full of a number of things," they were more triumphant than

[13] John Norris, *My Estate*, in *A Collection of Miscellanies* (4th ed.;
London, 1706), p. 60.

any king since Tamburlaine. With Henry More, they felt an "enlarg'd delight" as "unbounded joys" filled their "boundless minds,"

> an all spreaden love
> To the vast Universe my soul doth fit,
> Makes me half-equall to All-seeing Jove.
> My mightie wings high stretch'd then clapping light,
> I brush the starres and make them shine more bright.
> Then all the works of God with close embrace
> I dearly hug in my enlargéd arms.   (*Cupid's Conflict*)

Far from feeling that the new philosophy belittled man, as did many anti-Copernicans, poets, philosophers, and scientists found in it fresh evidence for the greatness of man, whose imagination could expand with the universe, whose soul grew vaster with vastness:

> A soul, capacious of the Deity,
> Nothing, but He that made, can satisfy.
> A thousand worlds, if we with Him compare
> Less than so many drops of water are.

The God of the new philosophy was a God of Platonic plenitude, but even more a Deity of telescopic astronomy and Brunoesque philosophy,

> Outreaching heaven's wide vasts, the bounds of nought,
> Transcending all the circles of our thought. . . .
> O King, whose greatness none can comprehend,
> Whose boundless goodness doth to all extent,
> Light of all beauty, ocean without ground,
> That standing, flowest, giving, doth abound.[14]

Old ideas of the release of soul from body came back with new meaning. In trance, in ecstasy and vision, the soul had

[14] Drummond of Hawthornden, *Hymn of the Fairest Fair.*

long traveled to the spheres, on Pegasean steeds poets had always mounted into space. Pegasus, trance, vision, ecstasy continued as devices in the seventeenth and eighteenth centuries, but more than one poet found release from finite limitations through Galileo's tube. As he sailed among the planets, he looked back at earth, seeing it in new perspective, as did Cowley in *The Exstasy:*

> I leave mortality and things below; . . .
> And lo! I mount, and lo!
> How small the biggest parts of Earth's proud title show!
> Where shall I find the noble British land?
> Lo! I at last a northern speck espy,
> Which in the sea dost lie,
> And seems a grain of sand.

Earth lost in the distance, the poet looked up to the heavens "through several orbs which one fair planet bear,"

> Where I behold distinctly as I pass,
> The hints of Galileo's glass.
> I touch at last the spangled sphere;
> Here all th' extended sky
> Is but one galaxy,
> 'Tis all so bright and gay,
> And the joint eyes of night make up a perfect day.

"The human understanding is unquiet," Bacon had said.[15] "It cannot stop or rest, and still presses onward. Therefore it is that we cannot conceive of any end or limit to the world, but always as of necessity it occurs to us that there is something beyond." Bacon had believed that the human understanding pressed on to infinity "in vain," but not so his followers. The *ne plus ultra* of an earlier period gave way to *plus ultra,* the most characteristic motto of the later seven-

[15] *Novum Organum,* Aphorism XLVIII.

teenth century. Man's world had shrunk, but he was less conscious of a narrow world than of an expanded universe. Finite in his body he was infinite in a mind that could soar "above those boundless bounds where stars do move." In that insatiability lay both his strength and his weakness, but for a time he was conscious only of greatness which he read into stars and planets, into space, and not least into himself.

v

"It is of the nobility of man's soul that he is insatiable," wrote Thomas Traherne. As Herbert embodied all the themes of the poets of content, Traherne was the seventeenth-century climax of the poets of aspiration. Mystic as he was, he seemed to the critics who discovered his poetry in the nineteenth century to have lived apart from his time in a timeless universe, as remote from the discoveries of his age as his own works remained for more than two hundred years. We know now that Traherne was deeply affected by the discoveries of the new science and the implications of the new philosophy. When he saw eternity in a grain of sand, he was speaking not only mystically but microscopically. The worlds unnumbered through which his God was known were his heritage from both the Platonists and the telescope. In the *Centuries of Meditations* he spoke metaphorically of the impact of learning upon him in his university days: "I saw that there were things in this world of which I never dreamed, glorious secrets. . . . There I saw into the nature of the Sea, the Heavens, the Sun, the Moon, and the Stars, the Elements, Minerals, and Vegetables. All which appeared like the King's Daughter, all glorious within."

But training in science and philosophy served only to heighten youthful intuition. Even in childhood he was engrossed with the two concepts that are most persistent in his prose and poetry: Eternity and Infinity. *"Infinite,"* he wrote, "is the first thing which is naturally known. Bounds or limits are discerned only in a secondary manner. Suppose a man were born deaf and blind. By the very feeling of his soul, he apprehends *infinite* about him, infinite space, infinite darkness. He thinks not of walls and limits till he feels them and is stopped by them. That things are finite, therefore, we learn by our senses. But *infinity* we know and feel in our souls." So too with Eternity. In youth he had taken for granted that the world was eternal. "Sometimes my thoughts would carry me to the Creation, for I had heard now, that the World, which at first I thought was eternal, had a beginning; how therefore that beginning was, and why it was, why it was no sooner, I mightily desired to know." He wondered, "How the Earth did end? Whether walls did bound it, or sudden precipices? Or whether the Heavens by degrees did come to touch it?" [16] That early sense of the Infinite and Eternal he never lost. "My inclination," as he said, "rais'd me up on High, and guided me to trace Infinity."

> I know not well
> What did me tell
> Of endless Space; but I
> Did in my Mind
> Som such thing find
> To be beyond the Sky
> That had no Bound.   (*Sight*)

[16] Traherne, *Centuries of Meditations*, ed. by Bertram Dobell (London, 1927), I.22; III.36; III.81; III.18; III.17.

> My Contemplation Dazles in the End
>> Of all I comprehend,
>> And soars abov all Heights,
> Diving into the Depths of all Delights.   (*The Anticipation*)

To Traherne, contentment *was* a sleepy thing. His soul was wide awake, conscious of its power to expand with the infinity and eternity in which he found the true felicity:

> Prompted to seek my Bliss abov the Skies,
>> How often did I lift mine Eys
>>> Beyond the Spheres!
> Dame Nature told me there was endless Space
> Within my Soul; I spy'd its very face:
>> Sure it nought for nought appears.
>> What is there which a Man may see
>>> Beyond the Sphere?
>>   FELICITY   (*Felicity*)

Like the earlier poets Traherne loved the symbol of the circle, but he used it in a different way. "I was an Adam there, / A little Adam in a Sphere Of Joys." He might see the circle in

> The Gem
>> The Diadem,
>> The Ring enclosing all
> That stood upon this Earthen Ball;
>> The heaven'ly Ey,
>> Much wider than the Sky.
> Wherein they All included were,   (*News*)

but for the most part his was not a sphere but a circle everywhere extended, the circle whose circumference is nowhere:

> I was an inward Sphere of Light,
> Or an Interminable Orb of Sight,

An Endless and a Living Day,
A vital Sun that round about did ray
    All Life, all Sence,
A Naked Simple Pure Intelligence.   *(The Preparative)*

A Strange Extended Orb of Joy,
    Proceeding from within,
Which did on evry side convey
It self, and being nigh of Kin
    To God did evry Way
Dilate it self even in an Instant, and
Like an Indivisible Centre Stand,
At once Surrounding all Eternity.
    Twas not a Sphere,
    Yet did appear,
One Infinit. Twas somwhat evry where.   *(My Spirit)*

His Omnipresence is an Endless Sphere,
Wherein all Worlds as his Delights appear. . . .
His Glory Endless is, and doth Surround
And fill all Worlds, without or End or Bound.

                            (Thoughts, IV)

The Herberts were content to remain in their well furnished tents, wherein they might lie warm and without adventure. The Trahernes were incapable of resting within finite limits:

This busy, vast, enquiring Soul
    Brooks no Controul,
    No Limits will endure
Nor any Rest.   *(Insatiableness, II)*

They did not disparage the world, but loved it for its fullness and diversity, its richness and beauty. It was

> A World of Endless Joys by Nature made,
> That needs much flourish ever, never fade.
> A Wide, Magnificent, and Spacious Skie,
> So rich tis Worthy of the Deity.   (*Nature*)

But they could not be content with one world or with one universe. "Farre aboven and aboven" their imaginations grazed in the rich pastures of an infinite universe, finding food for a very different satisfaction:

> My Inclinations rais'd me up on high
> And guided me to all Infinitie.
> A Secret self I had enclosed within,
> That was not bounded with my Clothes or Skin,
> Or terminated with my Sight, the Sphere
> Of which was bounded with the Heavens here.   (*Nature*)

They too had their cupboards of food and cabinets of pleasure —indeed the cabinet-figure is more frequent in Traherne than in Herbert—but they did not linger long in any one room of their vast dwelling-place:

> But yet there were new Rooms and Spaces more,
> Beyond all these, New Regions ore and ore,
> Into all which my pent-up Soul like fire
> Did break, Surmounting all I here admire.
> The Spaces fild were like a Cabinet
> Of Joys before me most Distinctly set:
> The Empty, like to large and Vacant Room
> For Fancy to enlarge in, and presume
> A Space for more . . .   (*Nature*)

Like Milton, Traherne felt an aesthetic gratification in the new space, though he went beyond Milton in his enthusiasm for the vast canvas of the Infinite Artist who must create pictures to infinity. "Infinity of space," he wrote, "is like a

painter's table, prepared for the ground and field of those
colours that are to be laid thereon. Look how great he in-
tends the picture, so great does he make the table." [17] But
even more than to the aesthetics he responded to the new psychology of infinity:

> I felt no Dross nor Matter in my Soul,
> No Brims nor Borders, such as in a Bowl. . . .
> We see: My Essence was Capacitie.   (*My Spirit*)

The capability of the human imagination to grow with the
universe, the capacity of the human soul to be filled yet still
to aspire for more beyond—such was Traherne's gospel:
"Objects are so far from diminishing, that they magnify the
faculties of the soul beholding them. . . . The whole hemisphere and the heavens magnify your soul to the wideness
of the heavens; all the spaces above the heavens enlarge it
wider to their own dimensions. And what is without limit
makes your conception illimited and endless." [18] The more
there was to know, the more the insatiable mind desired to
know it. The vastness of the new universe challenged imagination to an extent man had never known:

> The Ey's confind, the Body's pent
> In narrow Room; Lims are of small Extent,
> But Thoughts are always free.
> And as they're best
> So can they even in the brest
> Rove ore the World with Libertie;
> Can enter Ages, Present be
> In any Kingdam, into Bosoms see.
> Thoughts, Thoughts can come to Things and view

[17] *Centuries of Meditations,* v.5, p. 308.
[18] *Ibid.,* IV.73, pp. 279–80.

> What Bodies cant approach unto.
> They know no Bar, Denial, Limit, Wall:
> But have a Libertie to look on all.   (*Thoughts, I*)

"Where did we get this high and vast desire, / Unto immortal things still to aspire?" Drummond had asked. Traherne knew. In a new Infinite man was discovering new capacities. As philosophers were evolving a metaphysics of space, poets were building another aesthetics and an ethics to take the place of that symbolized by the closed circle. The new philosophy that had called all in doubt now gave back to man what should be his by nature—what had been Traherne's even in infancy. It released him from the limits of a finite world and universe, gave mind and spirit space to expand, afforded room to those thoughts that wander through eternity. Pondering upon vastness, the soul of man became vast. Its essence was "capacitie." Man was discovering a new aesthetics—the aesthetics of the infinite.

The "enthusiastick" poets uttered no lament of the Trojan Women when the walls of the world crashed down. Too long cribbed, cabined, and confined, their "pent up Souls like fire" consumed the barriers of the universe. They were the insatiable generation of whom Henry More—who had reason to understand them—said in his *Divine Dialogues:* "You are the most rapturous and ecstatical Company of People that I have ever met with in all my life; a kind of Divine Madness, I think, rules among you." Like More they were "drunk" and expressed their emotions in a language of excess. Traherne "felt a Vigour in my Sence / That was all SPIRIT. I within did flow / With Seas of Life, like Wine." He praised God, "For giving me Desire, / An Eager Thirst, a burning Ardent fire." "This Soaring Sacred Thirst" was the

"Ambassador of Bliss" making him "apt to Prize, and Taste, and See."

> No more shall Walls, no more shall Walls confine
> That glorious Soul which in my Flesh doth shine:
>> No more shall Walls of Clay or Mud
>> Nor Ceilings made of Wood,
>> Nor Crystal Windows, bound my Sight,
>> But rather shall admit Delight.   (*Hosanna*)

The "divine madness" was not only—indeed, not chiefly —a *furor poeticus*. The greatest exponents of aspiration were scientists who, in prefaces and conclusions to their scientific works, spoke a language as enthusiastic as Traherne's. "You, most Noble Souls, the true Lovers of Free and Experimental Philosophy," wrote Henry Power in the Conclusion to his *Experimental Philosophy* in 1664, "you are the enlarged and Elastical Souls of the World, who . . . do make way for the Springy Intellect to flye out into its desired Expansion." As he thought of the potentialities of his age he rose to heights of optimism, "corresponding" to the depths of pessimism to which Donne had fallen. "This is the Age in which all mens Souls are in a kind of fermentation, and the spirit of Wisdom and Learning begins to mount and free it self from those drossie and terrene Impediments wherewith it hath been so long clogg'd. . . . This is the Age wherein (me-thinks) Philosophy comes in with a Spring-Tide. . . . Me-thinks, I see how all the old Rubbish must be thrown away, and the rotten Buildings be overthrown, and carried away with so powerful an Inundation. These are the days that must lay a new Foundation of a more magnificent Philosophy." Scientists like poets sang hymns of praise to the New God of the New Universe; but their greatest paeans of praise were to Man. If they did not feel as fully as did the poets the aesthetics of the infinite, they were even more conscious of the psychology of infinity. The more they discovered about the new world and the new universe, the more insatiably they labored to tear down the rotten buildings and replace them with a grander structure. The more imagination strove to grasp the astounding new universe, the more truly man realized his own potentialities, and the vaster his soul grew with that too much that was not enough. Poets, scientists, philosophers of a newer "new philosophy"—these were the first Romanticists.

INDEX

Addison, Joseph, 5, 30
Advancement of Learning (Bacon), 9*n*, 25*n*, 124
Ages of the World, 92-94, 95
Agonie, The (Herbert), 179
Agrippa, Cornelius, 22
All Coherence Gone (Harris), 111*n*
Altdorfer, Albrecht, 24-25
Anatomie of Abuses (Stubbes), 26*n*
Anatomie of the World, An (Donne), 18, 81, 83, 90*n*; *see also Anniversaries, The*
Anatomy, *see* Physiology
Anatomy of Melancholy, The (Burton), 15, 25*n*, 34, 35*n*, 188-89
Anaxagoras, 136
Ancients and Moderns (Jones), 111*n*
Animism, 10, 21; dilemma of, 122, 129, 166, 167; Harvey and, 132, 134, 141; Gilbert and, 144, 145; Kepler and, 149, 150
Anniversaries, The (Donne), 81-108, 116
  First, 95, 96, 99-102, 107, 112-15, 120-21, 147-48, 156, 172
  Second, 19-20, 78, 94, 99, 102-7, 126-27, 128, 129, 146-47, 157
Anticipation, The (Traherne), 198
Antidote against Atheism (More), 39*n*

Aratus, 92-93
Aristotle, 118, 122, 131; heresy of eternity, 43, 161, 163; Milton and, 182; on origin of waters, 133, 137; Gilbert on, 145; astronomy and, 147
Art of the Renaissance in Northern Europe (Benesch), 22*n*, 25*n*, 54*n*, 65*n*
Ascher, Anita, 150*n*
Astraea, legend of, 92-96, 97
Astrology, 115, 119, 159, 169
Astronomy: Ptolemaic, 18, 28, 31, 50-51, 148, 186, 187; music of the spheres and, 29-30; Copernican, 31, 115-16, 119, 146, 151, 156, 159, 160, 171, macrocosm-microcosm analogy and, 35; Circle of Perfection and, 49, 51, 146, 147-48; *novae*, 116-19 *passim*, 156, 169; Christian tradition and, 118, 119-20, 122; Galileo and, 119, 156, 169, 171; Aristotle and, 147; elliptic orbits, 153-54; Herbert on, 179-80; Milton on, 184-87; proportion and, 189-92; poetry and, 194-95; *see also* Earth; Moon; Sun
Augmentis Scientiarum, De (Bacon), 9*n*
Augustine, Saint, 108, 118, 122